Žižek: Paper Revolutionary

POSTMODERN ETHICS SERIES

Postmodernism and deconstruction are usually associated with a destruction of ethical values. The volumes in the Postmodern Ethics series demonstrate that such views are mistaken because they ignore the religious element that is at the heart of existential-postmodern philosophy. This series aims to provide a space for thinking about questions of ethics in our times. When many voices are speaking together from unlimited perspectives within the postmodern labyrinth, what sort of ethics can there be for those who believe there is a way through the dark night of technology and nihilism beyond exclusively humanistic offerings? The series invites any careful exploration of the postmodern and the ethical.

Series Editors:

Marko Zlomislic (Conestoga College)
† David Goicoechea (Brock University)

Other Volumes in the Series:

Cross and Khôra: Deconstruction and Christianity in the Work of John D. Caputo edited by Neal DeRoo and Marko Zlomislić

Agape and Personhood with Kierkegaard, Mother, and Paul (A Logic of Reconciliation from the Shamans to Today) by David Goicoechea

The Poverty of Radical Orthodoxy edited by Lisa Isherwood and Marko Zlomislić

Theologies of Liberation in Palestine-Israel: Indigenous, Contextual, and Postcolonial Perspectives edited by Nur Masalha and Lisa Isherwood

Agape and the Four Loves with Nietzsche, Father, and Q (A Physiology of Reconciliation from the Greeks to Today) by David Goicoechea

Fundamentalism and Gender: Scripture—Body—Community edited by Ulrike Auga, Christina von Braun, Claudia Bruns, and Jana Husmann

Žižek: Paper Revolutionary

A Franciscan Response

MARKO ZLOMISLIĆ

POSTMODERN ETHICS SERIES 10

PICKWICK *Publications* · Eugene, Oregon

ŽIŽEK: PAPER REVOLUTIONARY
A Franciscan Response

Postmodern Ethics 10

Pickwick Publications
An Imprint of Wipf and Stock Publishers
199 W. 8th Ave., Suite 3
Eugene, OR 97401

www.wipfandstock.com

PAPERBACK ISBN: 978-1-4982-8349-6
HARDCOVER ISBN: 978-1-4982-8351-9
EBOOK ISBN: 978-1-4982-8350-2

Cataloguing-in-Publication data:

Names: Zlomislić, Marko.

Title: Žižek: paper revolutionary / by Marko Zlomislić.

Description: Eugene, OR: Pickwick Publications, 2018 | Series: Postmodern Ethics | Includes bibliographical references.

Identifiers: ISBN 978-1-4982-8349-6 (paperback) | ISBN 978-1-4982-8351-9 (hardcover) | ISBN 978-1-4982-8350-2 (ebook)

Subjects: LCSH: Žižek, Slavoj. | Haecceity (Philosophy). | Lacan, Jacques, 1901–1981.

Classification: LCC B4870.Z594 Z44 2018 (print) | LCC B4870.Z594 (ebook)

Manufactured in the U.S.A.   05/17/18

What sort of philosophy one chooses depends, therefore, on what sort of man one is; for a philosophical system is not a dead piece of furniture that we accept or reject as we wish; it is rather a thing animated by the soul of the person who holds it.

—Johann Gottlieb Fichte, *The Science of Knowledge* (1794)

Eventually, this present age tires of its chimerical attempts until it declines back into indolence. Its condition is like one who has just fallen asleep in the morning: first, great dreams, then laziness, and then a witty or clever reason for staying in bed . . . A Revolutionary Age is an age of action; the present age is an age of advertisement, or an age of publicity: nothing happens, but there is instant publicity about it . . . Nevertheless, some political virtuoso might achieve something nearly as great. He would write some manifesto or other which calls for a General Assembly in order to decide on a revolution, and he would write it so carefully that even the Censor himself would pass on it; and at the General Assembly he would manage to bring it about that the audience believed that it had actually rebelled, and then everyone would placidly go home—after they had spent a very nice evening out.

—Søren Kierkegaard, *The Present Age* (1846)

The true function of an intellectual, in my opinion, is obviously not to be the vanguard of society, but to call into question what is instituted, to interrogate and criticize what is. Not for the pure pleasure of criticizing but because without a distance from what is instituted there simply is no thinking.

—Cornelius Castoriadis

It is indeed on the side of chance, that is, the side of the incalculable *perhaps*, and toward the incalculability of another thought of life, of what is living in life, that I would like to venture here under the old and yet still completely new and perhaps unthought name *democracy*.

—Jacques Derrida, *Rogues*

Contents

Preface: Stinging Nettles

> In the world even the best things are worthless without those who make a side-show of them: these showmen, the people call great men.
>
> —Nietzsche, *Thus Spoke Zarathustra*, "The flies in the marketplace"

THE NAME ATTRACTED MY curiosity as I was searching the library for new books by Derrida. Before he became famous, his last name was written without the diacritical marks. These marks of pronunciation change the way the name is heard. Taken away to locked in a linguistic prison, the fettered marks make the Slovenian name less jarring to Anglo-American ears. There is an ocean that separates Z from Ž. Ž is sharp. It cuts. Ž is abrasive; a real Brillo pad and not Warhol's cut-outs that lack glory. Slavoj means glory. He does nothing but glorify the lost, the banal, and the obscene.

I came to Žižek through Lacan as I was writing my book on Derrida's aporetic ethics. It is a detour that maps my father's itinerary. Slovenia was the "Yugoslav" land of plenty. Slovenia was the stop made before my father went to West Germany to become a *Gastarbeiter*. Not yet Austria but far from Bosnia-Hercegovina, Slovenia was the Western outpost of Yugoslav Communism; a little Hong Kong in a sea of Titoism. At least the tidy streets gave off this illusion.

In 1989, as the train left the station in Villach, Austria and made its way across the border into Slovenia, the cleaning lady proceeded to dump the garbage she had collected out the window and onto the pristine Slovenian landscape. Was I witnessing a Lacanian act of defiance or the height of Titoist culture? What does this have to do with Žižek? It is a question of presentation and how what is presented is otherwise than it is. Forgive my Kantianism here.

If *Wikipedia* can be trusted, the Romans believed in the saying *Nomen Est Omen*—the name is a sign. Žižek should not be criticized for pursuing the destiny of his name. Žižek is the itch unable to find relief in swirl of the great capitalist abyss. The word "ŽiŽ" in my other Croatian language is the sharpness of something. Think here of stinging nettle. It once blistered my hands at my grandmother's farm. ŽiŽ is arousal. It is *jouissance*. Given the name, what other choice did Žižek have but to devote his time, energy, and talent to Lacan?

In the village café, watching Žižek on *YouTube*, some friends not well versed in Lacan exclaimed, "Šta ga jebe?" I will leave this phrase un-translated. Perhaps it will pop in Žižek's hotel microwave as a kernel of enjoyment. Nietzsche has taught us that the work of a philosopher bears witness to who he is. I approach Žižek's work in this Nietzschean manner. Nietzsche writes, "Gradually it has become clear to me what every great philosophy so far has been: namely, the personal confession of its author and a kind of involuntary and unconscious memoir."[1] Žižek has given us a great confession and given my Catholic ears, it is one that others have not heard very well. Perhaps they are too take in by his style to notice that all substance is lacking. I'm not sure why Žižek has been taken to be a serious intellectual capable of providing insight and guidance into the problems that face us today. When Žižek concludes, "Better the worst of Stalinism than the best of the liberal-capitalist welfare state"[2] the only reasoned response is to say, that Žižek does not know what it means to think. His insight is stupid. Why stupid? Žižek knows full well what horrors Stalinism has created and yet he insists that Uncle Joe is a better alternative than Uncle Sam. I prefer to take my chances with Amerika or better yet, Kanada.

The only truth that Žižek provides us is the truth of his own pathology posing as a philosophy that gives hope to those caught in the swirl of the capitalist abyss. That he has managed to convince tenured professors in the United States of his "truth" is not shocking. Imagine how many English professors and Cultural Studies professors teaching Marxism in American and European universities are "oppressed" living under the thumbs of the

---

1. Nietzsche, *Basic Writings*, 203.
2. Žižek, *Trouble in Paradise*, 164.

capitalist ideology. I am putting Lacan's teachings into practice here. Lacan's definition of successful communication is "I get back from the Other my own message in its inverted-that is-true form."[3] Žižek's words will be sent back to him in their true form.

For my part, I must follow my own signature. Before the Ottomans arrived our family name was Vuletić which relates to the wolf. Given the history of the region, there has always been a strange mix between Slavic paganism and Franciscan Catholicism.

The name Zlomislić means "malicious thinker." The name was given to my ancestors who fought against the armies of the Ottoman Empire that had invaded Bosnia-Hercegovina. They thought maliciously about the Ottoman attempts to pacify them. Think here of Greek farmers rising up against invaders who came to take what did not belong to them. This present book is my declaration of war against the ideologies that Žižek wishes to return us to. I will be defending Derrida's Franciscan orientation against Žižek's Stalinism. Here, I go to war against Žižek's call to repeat Lenin, Stalin, and Mao, as a viable solution to the problems of our time. Of course, it goes without saying that my analysis here is my own. I am writing as a citizen; speaking and writing as an individual and not acting as a representative of any College or Institution. I could not resist writing a book about resistance to the theorists from Ljubljana. As a Derridean, I know that a letter may not arrive at its destination so naturally I send this to Žižek as a gift of thanks. Enjoy!

Marko Zlomislić

Galt, Barrie, 2018

---

3. As quoted in Žižek, *In Defense of Lost Causes*, 269.

INTRODUCTION

The Postmodernity of Franciscan Haecceity

I THINK THAT MY cultural and academic history gives me a unique vantage point from which to analyze and critique Žižek's project. This vantage point is not held by Žižek's American, British, and Australian admirers.

I was born in Communist Yugoslavia in 1966. To be exact I was born in the Socialist Federal Republic of Bosnia-Hercegovina on land that historically belonged to Croatia proper before it was annexed by the Ottoman Empire, the Austro-Hungarian Empire, the Kingdom of Yugoslavia, and Tito's Yugoslavia. There is a reason why Croatia resembles an apple with chunks taken out of it. Its neighbors were very hungry and loved the Adriatic coast.

My ancestors fought against the invading Ottoman Empire; against Serbian Chetniks from Serbia proper who murdered my grandfather in front of my mother and her family in 1942. Under the Communist regime my grandfather, cousins, aunts, and uncles were tortured and imprisoned. So when I hear Žižek, Badiou, Hardt, and Negri, and their American followers tell me about the virtues of communism and its unrealized potential I have to say, "No Thanks!" Indeed, if these tenured radicals really want to live out the dream of communism I am sure that North Korea would accept them with open arms as propagandists or basketball players of the Great Leader. I see no need to leap into the frozen arms of Lenin or into the bloody hands of Stalin.

My father had the good sense to leave Communist Yugoslavia in 1970 and immigrate to Canada. Canada is my home. It was where I was raised and educated. I have lived, worked, and studied in Europe. Munich, Vienna, Paris, and Zagreb were my homes. The Catholic Franciscan tradition along with Jacques Derrida's thought and work informs how I read the history of philosophy. My mentors at University were Hindu phenomenologists, Christian existentialists, and Heideggerian atheists. I studied under Mervyn Sprung who worked with Nicolai Hartmann, Debrabrata Sinha who worked with Eugene Fink, the Scheler scholar Johannes Nota, and Zygmunt Adamczewski who studied with Heidegger. Most of all, my philosophical approach comes from David Goicoechea, my mentor and friend; a first-rate Kierkegaard scholar who introduced me to Derrida and medieval thought. In short, I was very fortunate to have been educated in Canada.

I am a Canadian Croatian Herzegovinian postmodern Franciscan who has read and studied the tradition that Žižek makes use of in his many books. I have no issue with his use of Lacan to explain popular culture. My students found his work analysis of Lynch and Hitchcock quite useful, though at the end of the day I think it is like using a screwdriver to mix cement. My issue with Žižek lies with his call to repeat the lost causes of communism. This is the main issue that I focus on in the pages that follow. No amount of Hegelian dialectics can turn this legacy into something worth saving.

The Franciscan friars murdered by Tito's Partisans at the monastery in the town of Široki Brijeg close to the village of Rakitno where I was born knew this. Sixty-six Franciscans were killed during and after World War II. That communism had no future was known by those in my village who took up arms to defend their families against those who would murder the future. Looking at Žižek's career unfold it is easy to see how he managed to seduce all the tenured radicals into their peer reviewed paper revolutions.

My book will also expand on Fichte's claim that "What sort of philosophy one chooses depends, therefore, on what sort of man one is; for a philosophical system is not a dead piece of furniture that we accept or reject as we wish; it is rather a thing animated by the soul of the person who holds it"[1] to examine Žižek's work.

Fichte returns us to a complex existential character analysis rather than a simple *ad Hominem* provocation. Fichte's insights can be combined with what Erving Goffman says in his *The Presentation of Self in Everyday*

---

1. Fichte, *Science of Knowledge*, 16.

Life. Goffman holds that the self performs its public front while hiding its real self, backstage. Backstage contains the aspects of behavior that are inconsistent with its front. For Žižek this means that he feeds from the very system that he criticizes.

In Žižek's case, in front, he presents himself as a subversive revolutionary Marxist, Communist, Lacanian champion of lost causes. Back stage he is a consumer of capitalist products, has accumulated wealth from his globe trekking performances and publications. The front is presented to us as a great reader of Hegel, Lacan, Derrida, Kierkegaard, and Kinder Eggs. The back stage shows so many inconsistent interpretations that there is not enough time or paper to look at them all. Indeed what do we make of Žižek's claim that "often I don't have the time to read the books about which I write."[2]

Paul Hollander's analysis is clear. He writes, "The reputation and celebrity status of Slavoj Žižek is among the reliable indicators of the decline of quality of academic-intellectual life in North America and Europe. His ideas are also emblematic of the paradox of the pursuit of meaning leading to meaninglessness . . . it is difficult to determine what if anything has made Žižek more acclaimed and different from the hordes of other adversarial intellectuals, social critics and 'tenured radicals' who populate departments of English and the social sciences at American and Western European universities."[3]

The best example of what Hollander says can be given by examining the statements of Jodi Dean who has written a number of books and articles using Žižek's insights. Dean wants to rethink communism as a future project "rather than equating it with Stalinist of Maoist past failures."[4] The 100 million murdered as a result of communism cannot be read as a "past failure." Such empirical proof solidifies the fact that communism has no future.

Dean received a BA (cum laude) from that great underprivileged proletarian university known as Princeton, "where she read Marx and Lenin while studying the Soviet Union." [5] One would think that studying the political and

---

2. Olson and Worsham, "Slavoj Žižek, Philosopher, Cultural Critic and Cyber-Communist," 272.

3. Hollander, "Slavoj Žižek and the Rise of the Celebrity Intellectual," 358. Dušan Bjelić's criticisms of Žižek are to the point. See his "Immigrants as the Enemy."

4. Interview with Dean, "Re-politicizing the Left," 79.

5. Ibid.

ethical travesty that the Soviet Union was would have resulted in a massive critique of that system. But no such critique was forthcoming from Dean who went on to do graduate work at yet another impoverished institution, Columbia, where she once again did a study of the Soviet Union.

Here is the issue. Dean is considered to be one of the best interpreters of Žižek's work and yet she confesses, "I'm actually probably one of the worst people to ask about political science. I'm in extreme radical political theory, so I'm not really sure about the major discipline."[6] This is a baffling confession. And yet, Dean is a tenured professor teaching students how to reclaim "the communist tradition of party, organization and solidarity for the present and future, reviving hope for a revolutionary overthrow of global capitalism."[7] This is priceless. Echoing Sheriff Bell from the film *No Country for Old Men*, "you can't make stuff like this up. I dare you to even try." Dean is not an expert in political science yet she teaches in the political science department at Hobart and William Smith, another great under-privileged American institution. Dean says that she wants a "new American communist party" that "would have to be revolutionary."[8] Imagine the hammer and sickle over the White House as those spies from the TV show *The Americans* ride their victory wave.

This is Dean's vision of how a neo-Communist Amerikan revolution would happen. In response to the question, "Could you describe what global revolution might look like?" Dean responds and the passage is worth quoting extensively: "I think you could start having kind of a combination of Occupy-like groups starting to run small towns or small cities in better ways. Place like Detroit, places without strong infrastructure and then combinations of strong pressure on the official political regime. At this point is it violent overthrow or not? I'm not sure. That's about as far as I can go."[9] Dean then goes into a scenario from *Fight Club*. She claims,

> I actually think that with about a million or a million and a half organized people, you could do something essentially like a coup in the United States. That would involve not a military coup but a take-over of a few major entities. For example, you have a million people on the ground in a couple of major places, let's say block-ading New York (bridges and tunnels), and occupy something

6. Ibid., 95.
7. Ibid., 80.
8. Ibid., 88.
9. Ibid., 89.

major in Washington. Congress would probably be better than the White House . . . So occupy that, and then combine with really well-organized UPS and Fed-Ex people who take control of supply lines plus about a hundred really well-placed hackers who cut off the financial networks, control the media apparatuses of what goes in and what goes out.[10]

This "imaging otherwise" is one of the most humorous things I have read in an academic journal. Dean believes that UPS, Fed-Ex, and hackers can bring communism to the United States. It is not the neo-liberal fantasies that are the issue in the damaged academic scape of higher education in the United States where Dean's ideas are actually taught. The issue is the fantasies of professors like Žižek, Badiou, Dean, and so many others who want to impose a communist horizon through "bloggish" means.[11] What we have in Žižek's and Dean's work on "political theory" are great examples of moral blindness, political vacuity and totalitarian leanings that are naïve to the core. Clearly, Žižek is not without his supporters and admirers. Most come from the United States and the United Kingdom, those two colonial empires of liberal capitalism.[12]

This is how Paul Taylor frames the issue, "Through is inimitable use of philosophical excess in the form of frequently offensive examples and dirty jokes, the Slovenian philosopher Slavoj Žižek has risen either to academic celebrity status or notoriety depending upon one's personal taste."[13] Žižek's academic celebrity or status or notoriety cannot be reduced to a matter of taste. Žižek's work is not judged on the matter of taste but on the basis of evidence.

Taylor uses the example of comedian Russell Brand who "shares Žižek's strategic use of ribald humor's excess as an ideological tool with which to critique the contemporary mediascape."[14] Clearly, Taylor is playing with silly putty while making such funny claims. Nick Cohen of *The Observer* called Brand's writing "atrocious: long-winded, confused and smug; filled with references to books Brand has half read and thinkers he

10. Ibid., 90.

11. Most of Dean's work reads like a blog entry. See Dean's blog "I cite" at http://jdeanicite.typepad.com/

12. For example, Glyn Daly, Rex Butler, Jodi Dean, Paul Taylor, Adrian Johnston et al.

13. Taylor, "Žižek's Brand of Philosophical Excess and the Treason of Intellectuals," 128.

14. Ibid., 129.

has half understood."[15] This is also an excellent description of Žižek's many published interventions.

The same zeal for Žižek's work continues in Matthew Sharpe and Geoff Boucher's *Žižek and Politics*.[16] They claim "it is Žižek's masterstroke to have successfully applied this psychoanalytic insight into human behavior to politics."[17] What is so masterful? Applying Lacan to politics has accomplished what exactly? Nothing. Exactly. The only person to have benefited extensively from psychoanalysis is Lacan himself, who managed to see about eighty patients per day under his famous short sessions. Needless to say, these short sessions made Lacan very rich.

Politics as a form of behavior can only be analyzed by Lacan or Žižek, not changed. Using Žižekian-Lacanian theory will not help the Aboriginals in Australia to be free from injustice. It will not help those who live in poverty in the United States. It will not alleviate the plight of the homeless in Canada or safeguard the rights of refugees.

Sharpe and Boucher make the following conclusive recommendation: "A renewed Western Left will have to involve engaged concrete proposals for how to change the world to institute a more just post-neoliberal order. A brilliant theory of ideology and the subject, such are present in Žižek's work, is a necessary part of this task."[18] Again, Žižek's theory of the subject lacks any valorization of the person and as such, it is deeply flawed.

When Žižek's claims are subject to analysis and argumentation it becomes clear that they must be discarded for the sake of justice and ethics. Žižek of course will claim that his "position is grossly misrepresented."[19] The Hegelian philosophy of the negative, Leninism, Stalinism, Maoism,

---

15. Cohen, "*Revolution* by Russell Brand review."

16. Sharpe and Boucher, *Žižek and Politics*. There are a number of factual errors to correct. Sharpe and Boucher claim that Žižek has written books in Serbo-Croatian. No such language exists. Žižek has not written books partly in Serbian and partly in Croatian. If he has written in Slovenian then his works have been translated in Serbian or Croatian but not into Serbo-Croatian. Of course, it is funny when Australians tell me which native language I speak. They go on to claim that Žižek has mastered all the works of the German philosophers and French theorists. *All* their work. Boucher's website at Deakin University claims, "He is also an expert on the work of internationally celebrated philosopher Slavoj Žižek." See http://www.deakin.edu.au/about-deakin/people/geoff-boucher. They claim "no-one has ever written books like Žižek." Here is one from a Franciscan Derridean perspective.

17. Ibid., 8.

18. Ibid., 233.

19. See Žižek, "What to Do When Evil Is Dancing on the Ruins of Evil."

etc., do not contain any form of emancipation worth following. On the contrary these movements and the geography of terror associated with them must be actively fought against for the sake of haecceity and justice. There is no emancipatory potential in Hegel or Lacan's thought because it fails to emancipate the single individual.

Why must Hegel's analysis be rejected? Simply put, it levels off the uniqueness of persons into a bland "we." His *Science of Logic* makes this clear. It is interesting that Hegel goes in the direction of *haecceity* but he abruptly withdraws as if afraid of the outcome. He writes, "Diversity lies upon the thing, but this diversity in its properties is the thing as reflected within something else."[20]

To put it in Hegelese, the ground of being is haecceity. Hegel, afraid of what haecceity entails takes the one-way road of universalism. He writes, "What exists has being, but something other than it at once shines forth within it. Here is a world of reciprocal dependence."[21] What shines forth as Hopkins reminds us is me. It is not as Žižek and Lacan would have it, some monstrous *objet petit-à* that grinds me down as I pursue it like the owl of Minerva into a propane flame.

Hegel like Descartes reduces persons to things. A person is never a "mere singular individual." Hegel continues, "Despite the fact that some singular thing is merely something singular it stands connected with something universal."[22] The singular is not connected to the universal like an umbilical cord. The universal is not the ground of the singular. But Hegel argues, and here he is very wrong, "singularity as (such exclusive) singularity is not a true determination of anything. We cannot posit ourselves as exclusively singular."[23] It is evident how totalitarianism is Hegel's philosophy well-armed. Hegel writes, "My singular activity thus arms itself with the necessary means with which to realize my universal general end."[24] Hegel is right to insist that "what is essentially in question is the content of belief." [25]Hegel's modernity cancels out the ethical stance of what can be called the late Franciscan Middle Ages. In the Franciscan thought of

20. Hegel, *Science of Logic*.
21. Ibid.
22. Ibid.
23. Ibid.
24. Ibid.
25. Hegel, *Lectures on Logic*, 67.

Roger Bacon, Duns Scotus, Ockham, and Bonaventure the person in all their multi-faceted uniqueness is the primary focus.

The answer to Roberto Esposito's question, "What is the essence of politics?" is clear.[26] The essence of the political is the haecceity of the person. Esposito explains that metapolitical is "the undetected presence of metaphysical presuppositions in political thought."[27] Esposito writes, "Aristotle's *Politics* contains theses deriving neither from practical philosophy nor from ethics, but rather from metaphysics, and, more specifically, from the idea of nature."[28] When Aristotle defines the human being in terms of substance and matter and form then this "dispositif" is "transformed onto the field of politics."[29] This causes the effect of reducing and excluding certain persons. It is the *polis* that rules over the citizen who remains its property.

This is why Levinas asserts that ethics is first philosophy. As Agata Bielik-Robson argues, "Just as God is unique and singular [*echad*], bearing a distinct Name, so is his creation: equally separate, singularized, and free to express itself in the particularity of the name."[30] It is clear why leftists like Adorno in *Negative Dialectics* attack "philosophical nominalism" and why communism murdered those who defended the rights of the individual. Adorno states: "[T]he individual cannot be deduced from thought [. . .] The subject lies under a spell from which nothing but the name of subjectivity will free it."[31]

The link between politics and metaphysics is ruptured when the haecceity of the person shatters the *demos*. Haecceity comes before the juridical *persona* so that persons are not reduced to mere things. Between the Greek *demos* and the Roman *persona* Franciscan haecceity asserts itself for the sake of justice.

Already in 1268 Roger Bacon in his *Communia Naturalium* argued for the pre-eminence of the individual. He claims that God created the world for the individual. Within the Catholic tradition this makes sense since salvation is for the individual and not for abstract essences or groups. The ultimate intelligible object is not the Aristotelian genus or species but the individual person.

26. Esposito, "The Metapolitical Structure of the West," 147.

27. Ibid., 151.

28. Ibid.

29. Ibid.

30. Bielik-Robson "The Promise of the Name," 18.

31. Adorno, *Negative Dialectics*, 163, 182.

The Franciscan philosophers such as Scotus, Occam, and Bonaventure, with their understanding of the incarnation develop a difference universalism that upholds the unique singularity of all flesh. This outlook led Francis to a radical love that echoed the love of Jesus. Francis developed a love for each individual creature. Scotus takes this position and develops the concept of haecceity or "thisness." While persons do share a common form and have equal worth and dignity, their "thisness" makes them irreducible and unique. This is my Franciscan critique of Žižek's work.[32]

Board meetings have a curious feature known as the in-camera sessions which happens after the regular meeting has concluded. The first formal meeting has the Chair following *Roberts Rules of Order* with the CEO presenting new business and accountants asking numerical questions. The in-camera session begins when the CEO and his secretary leave. Suddenly stiff lawyers and conservative accountants suddenly become jovial and animated. They are somehow transformed by the exit of the ideological Other. What needs to be said is said clearly, honestly and with conviction. The first session resembles a formal Catholic mass said in Latin. It is often grave and strange. The second session is forthright and lively like a meal one has with friends and wine.

Žižek's work has never been subject to an in-camera session. Yes, Laclau and Critchley have tried to go to war with the Slovenian thinker but they were acting like CEOs of their respective capital. With the exception of David Pickus, no one has really said what needs to be said both in response to Žižek's work and character as he calls for a return to a murderous ideology responsible for the deaths of 100 million people. The evidence of this Real has emerged in Žižek's homeland of Slovenia. After the downfall of Yugoslavian Communism, the crimes of Tito's regime were on display in 600 mass graves unearthed on Slovenian ground. The Communists used Slovenia as a base from which to murder all those who opposed Tito's "brotherhood and unity" lie.

In recent years, Žižek advocates for a return of Lenin's, Stalin's, and Mao's ideology as a way to combat capitalism. His appeal has taken hold among many tenured radicals in the United States, South America and Europe but for those of us who have lived through the truth of communism, it is clear that Žižek's work does not contain any sort of radical emancipatory

---

32. I explore this approach in more detail, of course, in my forthcoming book *Franciscan Postmodernity*.

potential, especially as it passes through the bowels of Lenin, Stalin, and Mao and the performances of Lacan.

Specialists in Slovenia claim that its mass graves give it the distinction of being Europe's Cambodia. No wonder that Žižek's fellow citizens in Ljubljana are appalled at his Hegelian reversals which mock the dead that communism has planted in Slovenia's forests, caves, mines, and ditches. There are so many still alive who bear the scars of these crimes against humanity. What would be a proper analogy to show how abhorrent Žižek's call to repeat Lenin, Stalin and Mao actually is?

Žižek like Judge Schreber is an unusual case. Of Schreber Freud writes, "He believed that he had a mission to redeem the world and to restore it to its lost state of bliss. This, however, he could only bring about if he were first transformed from a man into a woman."[33] Schreber writings reveal the hope that when he was transformed into a woman he would be impregnated by divine rays, thereby giving birth to a new race of men.

Žižek on many occasions had written that he wants to bugger Deleuze with Hegel or bugger Hegel with Lacan etc. We are supposed to understand this move as an example of high theory's delirium. Jan Jagodzinski argues that "The charges of 'inconsistency' or 'oscillation' means very little when addressing this question, since the very delirium of Žižek's style is meant to be explorative and thought provoking."[34] Is it not clear that Žižek suffers from an adherence to a chronic delusional system?

After Khrushchev's revelations about Stalinism in 1956 and the testimonies of Solzhenitsyn, Czeslaw Milosz, Osip Mandelstam, along with the research of Robert Conquest, A.J. Gregor, Paul Hollander, Vladimir Tismaneanu, Alex Inkeles, Anne Applebaum, Jan Patocka, etc., Žižek 's call to repeat Lenin remains anti-human and deplorable.

The promise to rescue humanity through a cleansing violence shows us that Bolshevik utopianism ends only in mass graves and unknown gulags. As Tismaneanu writes, "It was not institutional anarchy that led to the millions of deaths, but rather the structure of intimidation associated with Stalin's vision of a perfectly unified society and the need to cleanse it of its vermin. [. . .] Leszek Kolakowski is therefore right: communist nihilism is related to Dostoyevsky's demons contempt for individual rights and their reckless exaltation of the cathartic virtues of violence."[35]

33. Freud, *Standard Edition XII*, 16.

34. Jagodzinski, "Struggling with Žižek's Ideology," 1.

35. Tismaneanu, *Crisis of Marxist Ideology*, 47–48.

When Lacan declares that he is not a nominalist and that he rejects the nominalist (Franciscan tradition) which he argues "is effectively the only danger of idealism"[36] it is no wonder that Žižek and Badiou attach themselves to Lacan and Hegel. Dialectical Materialism means the death of the individual person. Tito's method in Communist Yugoslavia following Stalin was to kill those who upheld the dignity of the person. This is why 663 priests and nuns were murdered during Tito's reign of terror. Haecceity opposed totality.

How do we begin to understand Žižek? Perhaps by using the jokes he tells as a tool for analysis. Freud has taught us that the joker dresses his obscure thoughts in humorous guise to hide inhibitions. The following joke that Žižek tells reveals everything about his vast authorship. "Two men, having had a drink or two, go to the theatre, where they become thoroughly bored with the play. One of them feels a pressing need to urinate, so he tells his friend to mind his seat while he goes to find a toilet. 'I think I saw one down the corridor outside', says his friend. The man wanders down the corridor, but finds no W.C. Wandering ever further into the recesses of the theatre, he walks through a door and sees a plant pot. After copiously urinating into it, he returns to his seat and his friend says to him, 'What a pity! You missed the best part. Some fellow just came on the stage and pissed in that plant pot." Žižek 's explanation is "The subject necessarily misses its own act, it is never there to see its own appearance on stage, its own intervention is the blind spot of its gaze."[37]

It is clear, that Žižek has been urinating in a pot as he is called the Elvis of Cultural Theory, the most dangerous philosopher in the West, and Hegel's clown. Succinctly stated, while even a broken clock is right at least twice a day we do not use it to tell time. If we want to avoid the worst then it makes no sense to follow Žižek to Stalin's *Terminus*.

Kant has a great line in *The Critique of Pure Reason* that provides an answer to Žižek's attempt to resurrect dialectical materialism. It presents, Kant says, "the ridiculous sight (as the ancient said) of one person milking a Billy-goat while the other holds a sieve underneath."[38] Is this not Hegelianism at its purest? The substance one thought was being ejected into the bucket becomes another unexpected one.[39]

36. As quoted in Žižek, *Less Than Nothing*, 780.
37. Ibid., 34.
38. Kant, *The Critique of Pure Reason*, 197.
39. I committed a Freudian slip while writing this sentence. It read, "ejected into the

There is perhaps one more way of making sense of Žižek's work and fame. Aesop's story of the *Fox and the Monkey* is a perfect story that can be used to analyze how power is obtained. The story is worth quoting in full. I am sure that you will be able to draw all the necessary analogies:

"A Monkey once danced in an assembly of the Beasts, and so pleased them all by his performance that they elected him their King. A Fox, envying him the honor, discovered a piece of meat lying in a trap, and leading the Monkey to the place where it was, said that she had found a store, but had not used it; she had kept it for him as treasure trove of his kingdom, and counseled him to lay hold of it. The Monkey approached carelessly and was caught in the trap; and on his accusing the Fox of purposely leading him into the snare, she replied, 'O Monkey, and are you, with such a mind as yours, going to be King over the Beasts?'"

---

subject."

1

Žižek's Monstrous Politics

For it is not so great a trick to win the crowd. All that is needed is some talent, a certain dose of falsehood, and a little acquaintance with human passion.

—Kierkegaard, *The Point of View*

SLAVOJ ŽIŽEK'S LEADING QUESTION is how we are to reformulate a leftist anti-capitalist project in an era of global capitalism. In attempting to answer this question, Žižek often uses Kierkegaard's insights to add weight to his analysis of the problems associated with our social and political reality. Yet when one reads Žižek's work on Kierkegaard, one is struck by the great number of inconsistencies and errors that are generated. Žižek considers Kierkegaard from the point of view of the political in such a way that he avoids and negates the religious, but Kierkegaard is clear that if a proper politics is to exist, it must be grounded in real religious selfhood.[1]

The single individual, as Kierkegaard makes clear in *Two Ages*, is "an essentially human person in the religious sense."[2] Kierkegaard's views are directed by a religious notion of selfhood. Politics without this source is a form of despair. By failing to see ourselves as religious beings, we are in despair.

1. An earlier version of this paper was read at Trent University. I would like to thank Byron Stoyles, Dan Siskay, and Raphael Nawaz for their hospitality. The paper was also presented at the University of Toronto Kierkegaard Circle. I would like to thank Ivan Khan for his kind invitation. I also wish to thank the three anonymous reviewers for their comments. All remaining mistakes, of course, are my own.

2. Kierkegaard, *Two Ages*, 33, 96.

This despair cannot be the basis from which to transform the coordinates of our current position. These coordinates, according to Žižek, reduce us to consumers and clients who are caught in the narrow circle of the commodity and the neo-liberalism of dehumanized globalization.

Žižek does not accept "liberal democratic capitalism as the final formulation of the best possible society."[3] While the spirit of his critique is correct, the reality of his solution is monstrous and filled with terror. One can criticize capitalism and the many problems it has created without leaping into the loving arms of Lenin, Stalin, or Mao, as Žižek does. I think that Kierkegaard's philosophy provides us with a better alternative—a radical opening from which to re-think political theology from the position of the single individual to come. The program that Žižek upholds is not adequate for the transformation of society or self because it does not have a religious understanding of the individual. As such, Žižek's position is grounded in despair, not love.

I want to show that the best evidence for despair is found in Žižek's writings. My Kierkegaardian concern is that Žižek's analysis remains at the aesthetic level of immediacy and impulse while not progressing to the stage of real existential faith, what Kierkegaard calls Religiousness B, where authentic repetition is located. In Kierkegaard words, "Repetition begins in faith. [. . .] repetition breaks forth by virtue of the religious."[4] To be clear, I am not critical of Žižek because he does not share the same sort of Christian faith that Kierkegaard has. I am pointing out that Žižek has no real sense of what Kierkegaard is trying to say. In short, Žižek makes a travesty out of Kierkegaard.[5]

The Inhuman Crowd

> There is therefore no one who has more contempt for what it is to be a human being than those who make it their profession to lead the crowd. Let someone, some individual human being, certainly, approach such a person, what does he care about him; that is much

3. Žižek, *First as Tragedy, Then as Farce*, 88.

4. Kierkegaard, *The Concept of Anxiety*, 18. Kierkegaard continues, "In spiritlessness there is no anxiety. [. . .] It is a perfect idol worshipper. It worships a dunce and a hero with equal veneration, but above anything else its real fetish is a charlatan" (95). For a sustained analysis of Kierkegaard's existential faith, see Tebbutt, *An Examination of Kierkegaard's Existential Faith*.

5. This holds for Žižek's reading of Derrida's work as well.

too small a thing; he proudly sends him away; there must be at least a hundred. And if there are thousands, then he bends before the crowd, he bows and scrapes; what untruth! No, when there is an individual human being, then one should express the truth by respecting what it is to be a human being.

—Søren Kierkegaard, *Upbuilding Discourses*

When we usually think of repetition, we think of the mechanical in which the same thing happens perpetually. This repetition is boring and cannot give birth to an event. For Kierkegaard, repetition involves a reconciliation of the old and the new at the same time. It does not mean as Žižek claims, that the past can be erased so that we can start from "a zero point."[6]

Kierkegaard contrasts his notion of repetition with Plato's metaphysics of recollection and Hegel's metaphysics of mediation, showing how his concept of repetition takes us beyond Plato's recollection to a new future. He demonstrates how the Danish word *Gentagelse* contains religious, ethical, and metaphysical meaning. In Danish, *repetition* means "to bring out" or "to fetch," for *Gjen* means "again," *tag* means "day," and *else* means "getting," so the word means re-getting it again in a new way each day. Plato argued that recollection involves climbing up out of the cave and recovering the past truth that the soul knew before it fell. Platonic recollection recovers only what has been lost. As such, there is no real future within recollection. For Kierkegaard, repetition is a forward recollection that renews all things. It brings a future that is unexpected.

Kierkegaard argues against Hegel's mediation because it negates the past. Kierkegaard shows how Hegelian mediation does not have a true living past. Hegel's mediation remains quantitative and mechanical rather qualitative and truly transformative. Kierkegaard shows us how a reconciliation of the past can allow for a new future.[7] By arguing against the Platonic and Hegelian positions, Kierkegaard shows that neither can account for the truly new. Metaphysical necessity lacks the newness of the event that arises out of contingency and possibility. Kierkegaard shows if there is to be a truly free decision, it has to be based on a qualitative leap

6. See "Interview with Slavoj Žižek," 1–5.

7. In Kierkegaard's words from *Concluding Unscientific PostScript*, "Therefore the Hegelian cannot possibly understand himself with the aid of his philosophy; he can understand only what is past, is finished, but a person who is still living is not dead and gone. Presumably he consoles himself with the thought the if one can understand China and Persia and six thousand years of world history, then never mind a single individual, even if it is oneself" (307).

rather than a quantitative buildup of antecedents, such as the acorn becoming an oak tree. Kierkegaard's model of repetition ultimately is based on the incarnation and the notion of personhood that Žižek's Hegelian-Lacanian model lacks.

Žižek is fond of a portion of St. Paul's second letter to the Corinthians: "From now on, therefore we regard no one from a human point of view . . . if anyone is in Christ there is a new creation, everything old has passed away, see everything has become new."[8]

Whereas Kierkegaard reads repetition as the new, Žižek interprets repetition as "the gesture of sublimation, of erasing the traces of one's past."[9] Here Žižek retains a Hegelian understanding that Kierkegaard rejects. In this beginning afresh, from a zero point, Žižek writes, "there is also a terrifying violence at work in this uncoupling, that of the death drive of the radical wiping the slate clean as the condition of the new beginning."[10] Kierkegaard argues that repetition does not involve the erasure of the past, but a reconciliation with the past.

Žižek sees this uncoupling as work of revolutionary love that leads to "the creation of an alternative community."[11] Kierkegaard would be opposed to Žižek's position because it lacks responsibility. Kierkegaard's repetition is responsible because it recovers the temporal past to make it new.

Kierkegaard challenged the tradition of Greek ethics, even as it still held onto the privileged place of right reason. Kierkegaard knew that Hegel was really more Greek in orientation than Judeo-Christian. Kierkegaard clearly saw that harmony under the natural law of reason was still understood as more important than social justice for the single individual. In making his case, Kierkegaard drew on the insights provided by Amos, the first writing prophet who made a case for the single individual. Amos spoke for those who cannot speak for themselves. He spoke for the poor and for those who are suffering. He demanded social justice for those who were sold for silver and a pair of sandals. His call for justice was rooted in love. It did not contain the terror that Žižek recommends for transforming the world.

As a Hegelian, Žižek often laments the loss of the Absolute. As a Leninist, he believes in the value of violence. He writes, "Kierkegaard enjoins a

---

8. 2 Cor 5:16–17.

9. Žižek, *The Fragile Absolute*, 127.

10. Ibid.

11. Ibid., 130.

true Christian believer to hate the beloved himself out of love."[12] To practice love in Žižek's sense is to bring the sword and fire so that the coordinates of our entrenched liberal-democratic positions can be re-situated on a "new" Leninist ground.

In an essay entitled, "Only a Suffering God Can Save Us," Žižek claims that in Kierkegaard's "'triad' of the Aesthetic, Ethical, and Religious, one should bear in mind how the choice, the 'either-or,' is always between the two. The true problem is not the choice between aesthetical and ethical level (pleasure versus duty), but between ethical and its religious suspension."[13] He continues, "We are never safely within the Religious, doubt forever remains, the same act can be seen as religious or aesthetic in a parallax split which cannot ever be abolished."[14] What Žižek says about doubt may hold for the aesthete who lives in the temporality of the immediate moment, stained with superficial passion and lacking the passionate inwardness of faith. It may hold for the ethical person who does have passion but remains troubled. It may be true even for the person of Religiousness A, the mystic, who is passionate about infinite resignation. However, Žižek misses Kierkegaard's point that faith brings peace to our anxiety.[15] Faith allows the self to rest transparently in the power that sustains it.

The insights in *The Point of View* show how Žižek has done injustice to Kierkegaard's position. For example, Kierkegaard writes, "If the crowd is Evil, if chaos is what threatens us, there is salvation only in one thing, in becoming a single individual in the thought of 'that individual' as an essential category."[16] The whole of his "literary activity" turns "upon the problem of becoming a Christian in Christendom."[17] Christendom is defined as "the caricature of true Christianity, as a monstrous amount of misunderstanding."[18]

12. Ibid., 154.

13. Žižek, "Only a Suffering God Can Save Us." Here Žižek is misled by the terminological correspondence between Hegel and Kierkegaard. Given that Žižek is a Hegelian, when he sees Kierkegaard use words like *spirit, mediation,* and *self,* he automatically concludes that Kierkegaard is borrowing from Hegel.

14. Ibid.

15. Kierkegaard, *Concept of Anxiety,* 159.

16. Kierkegaard, *The Point of View for My Work as an Author,* 61. If for Kierkegaard "the prime condition of religiousness is to be a single individual" (127), then Žižek's Leninism removes all traces of individuality.

17. Ibid., 92.

18. Ibid., 77.

Kierkegaard argues, "Wherever there is a crowd, there is untruth."[19] From an ethico-religious perspective, "crowd stands for number."[20] The crowd as an abstraction "renders the individual completely impenitent and irresponsible, or at least weakens his sense of responsibility by reducing it to a fraction."[21] Kierkegaard argues that the individual as "the witness to truth" has "nothing to do with politics and must above everything else be most vigilantly on the watch not to be confounded with the politician,"[22] who engages in confusion and untruth. Kierkegaard's political theology is based on a responsible loving in the appropriation of the most passionate inwardness, which is truth.

The Kierkegaardian witness is to engage himself if possible with all, but always individually, in order to disintegrate the power of the crowd. This witness has a duty to rescue the individual from the assemblage of the crowd. Following Lacan's point that a letter always arrives at its destination, here is the postcard written by Kierkegaard for Žižek: "It is impossible to attack the system from a point within the system. But outside it there is only one point: a spermatic point, the individual ethically and religiously conceived and existentially accentuated."[23] Kierkegaard is clear. He is defending a certain conception of individuality. It is this individuality that Žižek wants to overthrow or dialectically diminish.[24] Kierkegaard will guide us to the next section, when he writes, "The individual is the category of spirit, of spiritual awakening, a thing as opposite to politics as well could be thought of."[25]

---

19. Ibid., 110.

20. Ibid., 112.

21. Ibid.

22. Ibid., 115.

23. Ibid., 129.

24. In Žižek's words, "What matters is not the miserable reality that followed the upheavals, the bloody confrontations, the new oppressive measures and so on but the enthusiasm events stimulated in the external observer, confirming his hope in the possibility of spiritualized political collective." See *In Defence of Lost Causes*, 108. This is clear evidence that Žižek has not understood Kierkegaard's position. Why should we embrace with "enthusiasm" a project that continued with its vicious degradation of persons? A study needs to be undertaken to understand why so many intellectuals have been taken in by Žižek's totalitarian formulations.

25. Kierkegaard, *Point of View*, 132.

Monstrous Politics

> The only "realistic" prospect is to ground a new political universality by opting for the impossible, fully assuming the place of the exception, with no taboos, no a priori norms ("human rights," "democracy"), respect for which would prevent us from "resignifying" terror, the ruthless exercise of power, the spirit of sacrifice . . . if this radical choice is decried by some bleeding-heart liberals as linksfaschismus, so be it!
>
> —Slavoj Žižek, *Contingency, Hegemony and Universality*

In a recent book entitled *The Monstrosity of Christ*, Žižek writes with characteristic wit, "There is only one philosophy which has thought the implication of the four words (He was made man) to the end: Hegel's idealism."[26] According to Žižek, Hegel as the thinker of Absolute Spirit has thought through the implications of the incarnation. Žižek uses Kierkegaard only to bring him back to Hegel, who swallows individual freedom. In the *Philosophy of Right*, Hegel is clear:

> The state is the actuality of concrete freedom. But concrete freedom consists in this, that personal individuality and its particular interests not only achieve their complete development but they also pass over their accord into the interest of the universal, they even recognize it as their own substantive mind: they take it as their end and aim and are active in its pursuits.[27]

In their emphasis on totality, Hegel and Žižek cannot do justice to the singularity of persons. As such, they cannot fathom the promise of the incarnation, which states, "All flesh shall be saved." But the significance of the incarnation for political theology should be evident. The incarnation with its focus on the body as love can rescue us from what Achille Mbembe calls "necropolitics" or the destruction of human bodies. Necropolitics, according to Mbembe, deploys weapons "in the interest of maximum destruction of persons and the creation of *death-worlds*, new and unique forms of social existence in which vast populations are subjected to conditions of life conferring upon them the status of *living dead*."[28] Instead of a politics of war, violence, and death, we might have a political theology that values all flesh in its singular uniqueness. This position is far removed from Hegel when he

26. Žižek and Milbank, *The Monstrosity of Christ*, 26–27.

27. Hegel, *Philosophy of Right*, 160.

28. Mbembe, "Necropolitics," 40.

writes, "The single person attains his actual and living destiny for univer-sality only when he becomes a member of a corporation, a society."[29] The corporation has a collection, and collective of bodies cannot be focused on the single individual. I think Emil Fackenheim is correct to point out that "any inquiry into the truth of Hegel's philosophy must confront its claims with the gas chambers of Auschwitz."[30]

A number of former admirers have pointed out the bankruptcy of Žižek's corporate position. Ernesto Laclau, an early supporter of Žižek's politics, now writes, "The more our discussion progressed, the more I re-alize that my sympathy for Žižek's politics was the result of a mirage."[31] Claudia Berger argues that Žižek's politics gives us a world "eternally ruled by a monstrous earthbound Lord, a world not open to human agency and political change."[32] Adam Kirsch observes that the louder Žižek applauds violence and terror, especially the terror of Lenin, Stalin, and Mao, the more indulgently he is received by the academic left, which has elevated him into a celebrity and the center of a cult.[33] By following Alain Badiou, who argues for "the eternal idea of egalitarian terror," Žižek succeeds in "selling us a new tyranny."[34] Žižek's thinking, to cite Hegel's words from his famous preface, is "the same old stew continually warmed up again and again." Žižek wants to bring Kierkegaard into this stew. Such a move is a classic example of Žižek's inversion that is presented to us as a profound and necessary alternative to the liberal-democratic position.

To be charitable, Žižek does make a number of necessary observa-tions. He shows how the present liberal parliamentary consensus precludes any serious questioning of how its order "is complicit in the phenomena it officially condemns."[35] Žižek shows us that we are given the freedom to

---

29. Hegel, *Philosophy of Right*, 201.

30. Fackenheim, "On the Actuality of the Rational and the Rationality of the Actual," 698.

31. Laclau, *Contingency, Hegemony, Universality*, 73.

32. Berger, "The Leader's Two Bodies," 75. Berger wonders how Žižek has gained royal status and "renown in the Western theory market." My answer, to cite the market wisdom from Bosnia-Hercegovina, is that Žižek is selling testicles as if they were kid-neys. See also the rejoinder by Hart, "Can a Judgment Be Read? A Response to Slavoj Žižek." Hart writes, "Žižek's account evades the messy and nasty complexities of history . . . Žižek has things backwards indeed upsidedown" (191).

33. Kirsch, "The Deadly Jester,"

34. See Johnson, "The Ruthless Mind of Slavoj Žižek," 122–27.

35. Žižek, "A Plea for Leninist Intolerance," 544.

question as long as our questions do not disturb the predominant political consensus. Here Žižek names Greenpeace, Doctors without Borders, and feminist and anti-racist campaigns, which are "tolerated even supported as long as they do not get too close to a certain limit."[36] I share Žižek's concern that "our daily experience is mystifying. [...] [T]he reduction of freedom is presented to us as the arrival of new freedom."[37] But I part ways when Žižek urges the reinvention of Lenin's legacy as a reinvention of truth.

Žižek argues, "To put it in Kierkegaardian terms . . . the idea is not to return to Lenin but to repeat him in the Kierkegaardian sense, to retrieve the same impulse in today's constellation."[38] For Žižek, the name "Lenin" stands for "the compelling freedom to suspend the stale existing (post) ideological coordinates, the debilitating *Denkverbot* in which we live."[39] Here we see Žižek's inversion at work again. Lenin, who silenced his enemies and had his opponents murdered, is presented as the person who allows for freedom of thought. Here is the evidence from Lenin himself, who writes,

> But we say in reply: "Permit us to put you before a firing squad for saying that. Either you refrain from expressing your views, or, if you insist on expressing your political views publicly in the present circumstances, when our position is far more difficult than it was when the white guards were directly attacking us, then you will have only yourselves to blame if we treat you as the worst and most pernicious white guard elements."

And

> We stand for organized terror—this should be frankly admitted. Terror is an absolute necessity during times of revolution. Our aim is to fight against the enemies of the Soviet Government and of the new order of life. We judge quickly. In most cases, only a day passes between the apprehension of the criminal and his sentence. When confronted with evidence criminals in almost every case confess; and what argument can have greater weight than a criminal's own confession.[40]

---

36. Ibid., 545.

37. Ibid. A good example would be the sign at the McDonald's drive-through that reads, "Pay how you want," with the catch that you only have three choices: cash, Interac, or credit card.

38. Ibid., 583.

39. Ibid.

40. Lenin, "Lessons of the Moscow Uprising."

Žižek is not repeating Lenin. He is replicating him. By going back to Lenin, Žižek argues, "we obtain the right to think again,"[41] and in doing so we will be in a position to "break the spell of global capitalism."[42] It is simply absurd to claim that Lenin can be repeated and that a utopian spark can be rescued from his writings. The utopian spark that Žižek claims to find in Lenin was never present. While Žižek calls for a repeat of Lenin, notice how he downplays the crimes against individual persons committed by Stalin and Mao. Žižek writes, "In spite of all its horrors, the great Cultural Revolution in China undoubtedly did contain elements of such an enacted Utopia."[43] And "the Stalinist . . . terror was a gesture of panic, a defense reaction against the threat to this State stability."[44] We have heard this type of "Yes . . . But" logic in defense of Fascism, and here Žižek repeats it for the monsters of the left. Žižek wants to retain the Leninist "Utopian spark," but what he fails to realize is this spark helped to light the fires of misery and oppression.

Žižek continues his Leninist observations in "Human Rights and Its Discontents,"[45] in which the absurdity of his position escalates. The Lenin who murdered those who disagreed with him is now the Lenin who would save us to think. Lenin, in Žižek's view, is now to become an educator. In Russell's words,[46] "Such education does not aim at producing any mental faculty except that of glib repetition. [. . .] From such an educational system nothing of intellectual value can result."[47] Glib repetition is the repetition that Žižek would have us return to, which is evident from his misunderstanding of Kierkegaard's position.

41. Žižek, "Plea," 553.

42. Ibid.

43. Ibid., 559.

44. Ibid., 565.

45. Žižek, "Human Rights and Its Discontents."

46. Russell describes his meeting with Lenin in 1920: "Lenin was cruel. Lenin had no respect for tradition. Lenin considered all means legitimate for securing the victory of his party [. . .] He thought the world was governed by dialectic, whose instrument he was. Lenin seemed to me at once a narrow-minded fanatic and a cheap cynic. He explained with glee how he had incited the poorer peasants against the richer ones, 'and they soon hanged them from the nearest tree—ha! ha! ha!' His guffaw at the thought of those massacred made my blood run cold" (Russell, "From Idea to Essay," 71).

47. Russell, Unpopular Essays, 39.

Žižek argues that the Leninist intervention should be "properly political, not economic."[48] My Kierkegaardian reply is that such an intervention must be based on economy—economy understood as the law of the Kierkegaardian house.

Kierkegaard's Housing Project

> Imagine a house with a basement, first floor, and second floor planned so that there is or is supposed to be a social distinction between the occupants according to floor. Now, if what it means to be human is compared with such a house, then all too regrettably the sad and ludicrous truth about the majority of people is that in their own house they prefer to live in the basement.

—Søren Kierkegaard, *The Sickness unto Death*

Kierkegaard uses the image of a house to describe our relational personhood. I can live in the basement as an aesthete. I can also move to the first floor and live there ethically. In the struggle to be either aesthetic or ethical, I can discover the possibilities of the second floor and, with infinite resignation, I can realize the limits of the temporal, the finite, and the relative and relate to the eternal, the infinite, and the absolute. Kierkegaard shows that infinite resignation is not enough. Faith is the double movement leap that enables one to live simultaneously on all floors of the house.

I think that Žižek misreads Kierkegaard. He fails to realize that the person of faith does everything within the coordinates of living on all floors of the house at once. His or her decisions are not merely aesthetic, ethical, or mystical. The person of faith makes a decision at each moment with a responsibility that takes all levels of the house into account. The person of faith, according to Kierkegaard, makes decisions at each moment with a responsibility that takes all the levels of the house into account. Žižek, with his emphasis on the aesthetic, simply remains trapped in the Lacanian mode of desire and impulse.

It is also clear that Žižek misreads the teleological suspension of the ethical. As Kierkegaard shows in *Fear and Trembling*, Abraham leaps from the relative to the Absolute with the belief that he will get back the relative. He is resigned to give up Isaac while believing that he will get him back.

According to Žižek, Kierkegaard reveals "the properly modern point of our meta-tragic situation . . . when a higher necessity compels me to

48. Žižek, "Plea," 554.

betray the very ethical substance of my being."[49] Žižek uses Kierkegaard to provide himself with a model for the militant act of revolution, but I think that Žižek's Kierkegaardian conceptualization of radical politics fails, because it fails to understand Kierkegaard's conception of faith and is ultimately at odds with Žižek's collectivistic political project. While Kierkegaard's emphasis on the single individual seems to cancel out the basis for community and politics, it is clear that he is opposed only to the levelling off of individuality, which forms "an abstract power and is abstraction's victory over individuals."[50] The collectivist project defended by Žižek would again result in a social totality where all sense of responsibility is negated and where totalitarian impulses once again take hold.

Žižek takes Kierkegaard's reflections on the teleological suspension of the ethical and reads them as an act of emancipatory terror capable of transforming the coordinates of our social reality. In Žižek's reading, the teleological suspension frees the agent to perform a proper revolutionary act. According to Žižek, this act of terror is to be embraced with all its catastrophic consequences.

The teleological suspension of the ethical becomes a political suspension of the ethical. This suspension involves the acceptance of terror. Žižek observes, "The pious desire to deprive the revolution of its excess is simply the desire to have a revolution without revolution."[51] Žižek's favorite example is taken from the film *The Usual Suspects* where Keyser Söze, upon finding his family taken hostage by a rival gang, proceeds to murder his wife and children. This frees him to carry out the work of revenge without fear of his family being harmed. In a similar fashion in the movie *X-Men: The Last Stand*, Wolverine kills Jean in order to save her. As he plunges his claws into her stomach, he confesses his love.

This decision to kill what one holds most precious is praised by Žižek as the ultimate ethical act.[52] He writes that this violence should not be seen as a display of "impotent agressivity turned against oneself" but as an act of radical freedom that "changes the coordinates of the situation in which

---

49. Žižek, *Did Someone Say Totalitarianism?*, 14.

50. Kierkegaard, *The Present Age*, 79.

51. Žižek, *Welcome to the Desert of the Real*, 28–29.

52. Žižek is fond of such statements. For example, he writes, "In spite of all its horrors, the great Cultural Revolution in China undoubtedly did contain elements of such an enacted utopia" ("Plea," 559). If the word *utopia* means "no place," what exactly is an "enacted utopia?" The enactment of a non-place?

the subject finds himself."[53] The terror of the act allows the agent to gain the space of freedom.

Žižek's fictional hero Keyser Söze is not the father of faith but a fictional Mafia boss who upholds the capitalist order that Žižek believes needs to be overthrown. Keyser Söze would agree with Milton Friedman that the social responsibility of business is to increase its profits. Söze strikes at his own so that his profits will increase.[54] The cold-blooded calculation favored by Žižek cannot be found in Kierkegaard's position. Žižek's revolutionary subjectivity rests on terror, and as such, it cannot respect the singularity and uniqueness of persons.

The most profound expression of repetition, according to Kierkegaard, is "atonement."[55] To atone is to reconcile, "to bring together again," "to make reparation." How would Lenin and Stalin ever atone for the crimes they committed? How would they make amends? Žižek wants Lenin to be saved and redeemed. As such, there can be no reparation for Lenin's victims but only for Lenin himself. The tone of such atonement does not ring true because it is fall back into un-freedom. Kierkegaard argues, "In the individual, then, repetition appears as a task for freedom in which the question becomes that of saving one's personality from being volatilized and, so to speak, in pawn to events."[56]

Unlike Kierkegaard's single individual, Žižek's Lacanian subject of the gaping Real is an expression of the tormented psyche that can find no rest. It seeks to fill the gap of its misunderstanding with obscene pathological fantasies. This obscene underground domain cannot be transformed by a repeat of Lenin, especially when Lenin's so-called utopia became a nightmare whose blueprint still stains the ground in current world events. In reading Žižek's declarations, one shudders at the fact that such theorizing rests on a foundation of horror. Such theorizing has already produced tens of millions of bodies. In Žižek's words, "I am a good Hegelian. If you have a good theory, forget about the reality."[57]

---

53. Žižek, *The Fragile Absolute*, 150.

54. Žižek provides a number of examples of "striking at oneself," which all seem to be at odds with his political program. See *Fragile Absolute*, 149–53.

55. Kierkegaard, *Postscript*, 313.

56. Ibid., 315.

57. See O'Hagan, "Interview with Slavoj Žižek." Do Žižek's own words, "For me, always it is Hegel, Hegel, Hegel," suffice for those who cling to the idea that he is a Marxist-Lacanian?

In *The Ticklish Subject* Žižek approves of Brecht's *The Measure Taken*, the story of a youth who agrees to be murdered by his comrades for compromising their mission.[58] Žižek sees the murder of the youth as a sacramental event that is on par with the tenderness of the *Pietà*. Brecht's teaching play *Lehrstuck* is proof for Žižek that the Stalinist politician carries out purges, opens gulags, and engages in murder for the love of humanity. Given the spirit of existentialism, permit me a personal example. Unlike Žižek, who was not shot at and who did support the state apparatus in Yugoslavia, I have seen the results of his so-called revolutionary tenderness in mass graves throughout Croatia and Bosnia-Hercegovina.[59] To repeat Lenin, as Žižek urges, would be to increases the catastrophe rather than diminish it. It would mean to prolong the famine in so-called great leaps forward rather than find solutions to poverty and hunger. Žižek would have us turn up the volume on ruin while turbo-charging the speed of terror, all for the "love of humanity."

Conclusion

It is clear that Žižek's program masquerades as a concern for community and justice while it works to destroy the foundations of genuine community envisioned by Kierkegaard. When Žižek and Badiou urge a repeat of Lenin and Mao from the confines of their petit-bourgeois universities, their call is obscene and unwanted by those who know what suffering is.[60]

Kierkegaard's defence of the single individual is an efficient critique of the violent and totalitarian kernel of Žižek's politics. Kierkegaard's political

---

58. Žižek, *The Ticklish Subject*, 379–80.

59. Žižek argues that his reference to Lenin serves "as the signifier of the effort to break the vicious circle of these false options" ("Plea," 566). Žižek continues with his Lacanian reading, claiming there is "in Lenin more than Lenin himself" (266). So "to repeat Lenin is not to repeat what Lenin *did* but what *he failed to do*, his missed opportunities" (266). The logical question to ask is what exactly Lenin failed to do. Is Žižek advocating a kinder, gentler state-sponsored terrorism: Lenin with an excessive generosity? Between 1917 and 1959, over 60 million people were murdered in the Soviet Union. While this is not a scholarly argument, it is a practical and ethical argument against a repeat of Lenin. For the Left, these numbers are acceptable because, following Badiou and Žižek, they were a necessary outcome of what Badiou calls the "Truth-Event known as the October Revolution." A repeat of Lenin would be nothing more than a retread. Tires that are re-treaded blow up quickly. Here I follow Aquinas who writes, "Useless repetition is vain."

60. I think that Fichte was correct when he maintained that the kind of philosophy a person has shows the kind of person he or she is.

theology can be found quite clearly in *Two Ages*. There Kierkegaard argues, "Not until the single individual has established an ethical stance despite the whole world, not until then can there by any question of genuinely uniting."[61] If Kierkegaard has a negative evaluation of the political, it is because the political has not taken the single individual into account.

What is the relevance of Kierkegaard's politics vis-à-vis today's secular, democratic, emancipatory, and globalist ethos? Today's secular politics is not emancipatory or democratic. Current politics has embraced power and violence and has not practised compassion, love, or forgiveness.

Here a reading of Kierkegaard's *Works of Love* as a political text would bring out a politics of love for the neighbour. Kierkegaard's critique of the crowd is applicable today as a response to both Hardt and Negri. The multitude cannot act responsibly toward the other. It cannot forgive or display compassion. It displays force and revenge.

Kierkegaard makes clear that love of neighbor is not love of humanity. The single individual does not exist in "humanity." Love of neighbor is love of every other individual, not a love of all others collectively. Having reached the stage of real faith or Religiousness B, the single individual cares for the neighbor in acts of love for every other. Such a move is missing in Žižek's work. Kierkegaard, with his emphasis on the single individual, is not opposed to community. He is opposed to a false sense of community that eradicates all sense of individual existence. The evidence is clearly visible in mass graves and gulags.

If the self is a relation that relates itself to itself and rests transparently in the power that established it, then despair is a mis-relation in a person's innermost being.[62] For Kierkegaard the politics upheld by Žižek is a levelling off into a "monstrous abstraction as an all encompassing something that is a nothing, a mirage."[63] Žižek's politics delivers us over to despair. It is the politics of the enclosed reserve. As Kierkegaard writes in *Works of Love*, "What horror more terrible than if you had fallen among wild beasts for I wonder if even the wild nocturnal howling of bloodthirsty beasts is as horrible as the inhumanity of a raging crowd."[64] Kierkegaard's politics performs the works of love for all individuals who live and exist

---

61. Kierkegaard, *Two Ages*, 62.
62. Kierkegaard, *Sickness unto Death*, 49.
63. Kierkegaard, *Two Ages*, 90.
64. Kierkegaard, *Works of Love*, 169.

throughout the house. Love builds from the ground up.[65] Despair grinds one down. It is against this background that we can finally understand what Žižek means when he writes in *Violence*, "If one means by violence a radical upheaval of the basic social relations, then, crazy and tasteless as it sounds, the problem with historical monsters who slaughtered millions was that they were not violent enough. Sometimes doing nothing is the most violent thing to do."[66]

65. Ibid., 216.
66. Žižek, *Violence*, 216.

2

The Slime of Ideology

A state, is called the coldest of all cold monsters. Coldly lieth it also; and this lie creeps from its mouth: "I, the state, am the people."

—Nietzsche, *Thus Spoke Zarathustra*, "Of the New Idols"

ERNESTO LACLAU'S INTRODUCTION TO Žižek's *The Sublime Object of Ideology* mentions the distinctive features of Žižek's use of Lacan. First, Žižek and his Slovenian school use Lacan's theories to refer "to the ideological-political field." Second, Žižek uses Lacan to analyze classical philosophical texts. Both these moves take Lacan out of his main clinical context. Žižek's theoretical interventions insofar as they rely on the Lacan's theories do nothing but return us to the dominant ideology of the master. The task of "constructing a democratic socialist political project in a post-Marxist age" is a return to Gulag politics. For those of us who have seen and witnessed the legacies of Marx, Lenin, and Stalin, Žižek's use of "Lacanian conceptual apparatus as a tool in the analysis of ideology" is comparable to the recent phenomenon of "pimping one's ride." Here four cylinder Hondas are re-tooled with massive mufflers that make a race car sound only to travel at tractor speed.

Laclau cautions us that Žižek's books do not involve "a systematic structure in which an argument is developed according to a pre-determined plan."[1] Žižek's style is described as "a series of theoretical interventions."[2]

1. See Ernesto Laclau's preface to Žižek, *Sublime Object of Ideology*, xii.
2. Ibid.

These interventions cannot achieve a theoretical fusion, because following Lacan, Žižek see the subject as a subject of lack. The materialism that Žižek upholds is reductionist and does not uphold the dignity of the person. Laclau sees Žižek as "constructing a democratic socialist project."[3] This project does not allow for the flourishing of singular persons. Though Laclau is perceptive in his critique of Žižek I do not follow his thought that "constructing a People is the main task of radical politics."[4] The main task is to uphold the dignity of persons. People do not need to be constructed since they already are.

Žižek sees a three-fold aim for what he is attempting to do. He wants to introduce the fundamental concepts of Lacanian psychoanalysis in order to locate Lacan "in the lineage of rationalism."[5] Žižek sees Lacan's work as "the most radical version of the Enlightenment."[6] Next, Žižek wants to accomplish a "return to Hegel" This means to "re-actualizse Hegelian dialectics by giving it a new reading on the basis of Lacanian psychoanalysis."[7] Finally, he seeks to "contribute to the theory of ideology via a new reading of some well-known classical motifs."[8] Here Žižek reads Marx through a Lacanian filter.

While arguing that the only way to save Hegel today is through Lacan and that this reading of Hegel opens a new approach to ideology, I will argue that this move has no regard for the uniqueness of persons. I begin with the extraction of key points from Žižek's text.

In defining ideology, Žižek argues that the kind of reality we find ourselves in "is possible only as the condition of the individuals partaking in it is not aware of its proper logic."[9] Ideology always reveals its true nature in the corpses that it leaves behind. If the arithmetic is correct communism left behind 100 million corpses. Notice the way Žižek frames his argument. He writes, "The very ontological consistency implies a certain non-knowledge of its participants—if we come to 'know too much'; to pierce the true function of social reality, this reality would dissolve itself."[10] Those who knew

3. Ibid, xv.
4. Laclau, "Why Constructing a People."
5. Zizek, *Sublime Object of Ideology,* xxx.
6. Ibid.
7. Ibid.
8. Ibid.
9. Ibid., 15.
10. Ibid.

too much, i.e., those who knew the reality of what was going on in the bliss created by Lenin, Stalin, Mao and Pol Pot, were murdered. This evidence is clear and distinct in both smell and substance. It shows us that the architects of the totalitarianism that Žižek's work defends knew what they were doing. Dissenters were dissolved. Lenin, Stalin and Mao enjoyed their symptom with full knowledge of its logic, trajectory and outcome.

While Žižek returns to Marx to give, "the most elementary definition of ideology" from *Capital*, namely: "Sie wissen das nichts, aber sie tun-They do not know it, but they are doing it," we must counter this epistemological stupidity with its opposite formulation: "They know what they do, but they tell you that you did it and that you are responsible." This is not the gesture of saying that the emperor has no clothes. It is the ethical insight that Marxist ideology to use the Bosnian phrase is "selling testicles as if they were kidneys" after having castrated its own loyal comrades. In this decisive step forward we have established a new way to read ideology. Ideology consists in the very fact that people do know exactly what they are doing.

To make this point clear we can examine Miguel de Unamuno's story, "San Manuel" (1931). The story introduces us to an atheistic priest who willingly deceives his own parishioners. While preaching about belief in God and immorality, San Manuel knows that religion is a fiction. This clearly shows how ideological beliefs are propagated while being incompatible with one's innermost beliefs. Manuel's motives are selfish rather than altruistic. Ideology is the creation of a world that serves the enjoyment of the Master. After the fiction is revealed for what it is, one is left with the feeling of being duped. Indeed one wonders how the fiction can be sustained for extended periods of time. Think here of CEOs who earn millions (doing what exactly?) while children starve. Think of how Chairman Mao lived in luxury while his comrades made the great march forward into famine.

When I visited Croatia and Bosnia-Hercegovina in 1989 while these countries were still under the Yugoslav ideological illusion, the everyday adherence to stupidity was made clear. Entering the train station in Mostar, I was greeted with a huge portrait of Marshall Tito. The extent of the Slovenian dictator's gaze over the people even after his death was priceless. The illusions were sustained. Those who spoke the truth and saw through the illusion were murdered by Tito's secret police (UDBA). Manuel sells the illusion to uphold the cohesion of the village. He manipulates so well and is believable due to "the effect of his presence, of his gaze and above all his voice."[11] Manuel like all masters has a commanding presence, a penetrating gaze and a divine voice. Does this not describe Žižek's performances, especially when hundreds gather round him and sit at his feet? See his performance in Buenos Aires as an example.[12]

Manuel wants the village to be happy and satisfied. He keeps them away from the truth that sadness brings. He claims, that the truth "is perhaps something so unbearable, so terrible, something so deadly that simple people could not live with it."[13] To make happy through the dream of immorality is already to deny life. The main thing is not to live but to live without illusions. Manuel claims that what he does is "for the people." This phrase echoes through all political ideologies and must be seen for what it is, namely a lie. Manuel's Leninism is clear, "It is better for them to believe everything, even things that contradict one another, than to believe nothing. Let us not protest". He continues, "Let them console themselves for having been born, let them live as happily as possible in the illusion that all this has a purpose."[14] Manuel quotes Marx's phrase "religions is the opium of the people" and concludes, "Yes, opium it is. We should give them opium and help them to sleep and dream."[15]

Manuel drives for happiness but it only leads to tedium and weariness. Manuel believes that "the people should be allowed to live with their illusions."[16] Manuel functions like a Tibetan prayer wheel. It prays while the villagers can do their work. If the villagers believe through Manuel who does not believe they are in situation of objective dis-belief. Manuel is like a paid weeper; women who are hired at funerals to save us from "the fright of real tears." Canned laughter however packaged is not funny, and fake tears are not sorrowful. How can the "as if" be overcome? To act "as if" we believe in God, the Party, the State, Communism, the reign of Capital is to live a life of deception. Žižek claims that "the function of ideology is not to offer us a point of escape from our reality but to offer us the social reality itself as an escape from some traumatic real kernel. The traumatic real kernel is ideology itself. It is traumatic when we find out that it was presented to us as real. In terms of ideology, the only escape worthy of the

11. Unamuno, *Abel Sanchez*, 212.

12. See, for example, the documentary *Zizek!* (2005) directed by Astra Taylor.

13. Unamuno, *Abel Sanchez*, 237.

14. Ibid.

15. Ibid.

16. Ibid.

name is from the illusion presented as the thing, movement, fad, belief to be followed without question."[17]

Žižek argues that "the dimension of truth is opened through our misrecognition of the traumatic Thing, embodying the impossible jouissance."[18] Žižek gives us the example of Ridley Scott's film *Alien*. He writes, "Is not the disgusting parasite which jumps out of the body of poor John Hurt precisely such as symptom . . . a sprout of enjoyment, a leftover of the maternal Thing?"[19] The interesting question is why did John get hurt? Did his desire to come into the depths of the Mother alien cause his destruction? The connection between *Alien* and Kant's essay *What is Enlightenment?* is clear. We must not allow ourselves to be the other's catch. The imperative to obey is the anti-Enlightenment stance of domination and the constant surveillance of the domicile.

According to Žižek, Lacanian communication occurs when "the speaker gets back from the recipient his own message in its inverted—that is—true meaning."[20] Žižek gives the example of a mother who complains that her family exploits her and that she suffers without reward. Žižek, following Lacan, believes that the mother's groaning really means, "Keep on exploiting me! My sacrifice is all that gives meaning to my life!" The Lacanian answer is that "the mother actively sustains the social-symbolic network in which she is reduced to playing such a role."[21] Žižek concludes in a very religious manner here. He writes, "We must conceive ourselves as formally responsible-guilty for it."[22] This acknowledgement that we are guilty for what the other bestows on us is precisely the royal road to the Gulag where the victim is responsible/guilty for having been victimized. This model can be given a precise formulation: the master is omnipotent while I am impotent. The elephant confined by a piece of twine needs only to pull free. Why it chooses to pull the Master's phallus for a few bales of straw requires much more careful reflection.

Taking Freud's description of the dream as a rebus, Muller and Richardson argue that "Lacan's own message is locked up in an expression so obscure and enigmatic that for the uninitiated it constitutes a kind of rebus

---

17. Žižek, *Sublime Object of Ideology*, 45.

18. Ibid., 79.

19. Ibid.

20. Ibid., 216.

21. Žižek, "The Big Other."

22. Ibid.

in itself."[23] A guide should at least guide us but Richardson and Muller's text fails to offer any clear path through the obscurity that constitutes most of Lacan's work. In defining Lacan's work as a rebus they "suggest that it is dealing with a theme that of its very nature escapes the constrictions of rational exposition"[24] Such an explanation is not helpful for it states that rational exposition constricts Lacan's mystical insights into the nature of the unconscious. We are told, "Lacan not only explicates the unconscious but strives to imitate it."[25] Given Lacan's thesis that the unconscious is structured like a language we must ask what Lacan is actually imitating other than deliberate ambiguity masking itself as profound pronouncements.

Contrary to Richardson's claim that obscurity is a sign that there is a significant meaning, I want to maintain that what is difficult should be made clear. Notice the religiosity of their advice. They write, "We are convinced that Lacan has something to say that is worth hearing . . . .in order to gain access to whatever hidden wealth is here, an extraordinary ascesis is necessary."[26] Why must this be the case? The drug user who claims to see God is simply on drugs. The monk locked in his cell without adequate food or water; whipping himself will only arrive at the truth of his own depraved condition. The Buddha clearly showed that ascesis is no road to enlightenment.

Richardson and Muller want to provide us with tools to unearth the gems in Lacan's text. But they claim, "it would be unfair to expect too much from a set of tools."[27] This rhetoric of failure is disconcerting. I expect the hammer to drive the nail. Lacan and Lenin would maintain that my fist can double as a hammer and that the nail I am attempting to pound with it cannot penetrate the concrete that Mao's *Red Book* says is really wood. The intent here is to turn on the light, "in the dark inscrutable world of the Lacanian rebus."[28]

While Rex Butler may be correct in asserting that "concepts can only be grasped through their examples,"[29] the examples chosen by Žižek to explain concepts are symptoms of hysterical babble that refuses to take direct

23. Mueller and Richardson, *A Reader's Guide to "Ecrits,"* 2.

24. Ibid.

25. Ibid.

26. Ibid.

27. Ibid., 25.

28. Ibid.

29. See editor's preface of Žižek, *Interrogating the Real*, xiv.

action when such action could have been taken. Žižek wants to challenge, "what passes in American cultural criticism for Lacanian theory." He argues that such work is "very limited and distorted." He wants to "render palpable another dimension of Lacan far more productive for critical social theory."[30]

How can Lacan's insights be harnessed as a critique of social theory when they were formulated as a response to patients under his care? How productive is Lacanian analysis for critical social theory? An understanding of his *objet petit-à* does not help municipalities to deal with sewer problems or traffic issues. Yet, Žižek and others would have us believe that Lacanian theory is quite effective. Notice the mountain of books, conference papers, lengthened CVs that have arisen as a result of Lacan's insights. Yet there is no measurable decrease in suffering since Lacan and Žižek and their followers have started publishing their great insights. Lacanian analysis remains an academic exercise; masturbatory in its essence without a revolutionary kernel that can transform the sorry state of human culture today.

In an interview with Eric Laurent, Žižek shows how he upheld the existing totalitarian order in Yugoslavia. Žižek tells Laurent that self-management, "lends itself to an explicitly Lacanian political analysis."[31] Laurent is wrong to conclude that self-management was not characterized by "direct oppression." The Yugoslav system was a paradigm of oppression from the beginning. Žižek supported a regime that oppressed millions of citizens. Of course he did not complain. How oppressed was he when he tells Laurent that his Lacanian group received, "State grants for our publications." In addition, his group had, "the ability to publish books, to organize public gatherings, colloquia etc." Such "toleration" was granted to those who were active members of the Yugoslav Communist Party. Those who did attempt to publish books not in accord with the Titoist Party line were imprisoned or assassinated. The Yugoslavian prison located at Goli Otok, (an island in the Adriatic Sea) was the place were those against the Party were re-educated by the UDBA (Yugoslav Secret Police). Žižek reveals his political stance very clearly. In the West he complains loudly about how bad life was for him in Yugoslavia, yet while living there he was living like a Lacanian master in a state-funded apartment.

Of course, one answer might be *pace* Richardson that the Yugoslav Communists could not understand what Žižek was writing. Why would they care? They were living like rich landowners while preaching the myth

30. Ibid, 250.
31. Ibid., 29.

of brotherhood and unity to those they enslaved. One of the biggest capitalists of all was the Slovenian Marshall and dictator of Yugoslavia, Josip Broz Tito whose opulent lifestyle could put the best capitalist exploiters in the West to shame.

When the un-educated communist cadre entered the village where I was born they initiated collectivization. All livestock and property were to be held in common. The results of course were disastrous. The wise peasants knew the truth and they spoke it saying, "Why would my neighbour get up at 5 am to milk my cow when he could sleep with his wife instead?"

Do we follow Žižek and find the truth of our situation in the parallax view which is the gap between two perspectives? To be free, our freedom must do more that persist in the space between the phenomenal and the noumenal. This betweeness is not freedom but misery.

The psychoanalyst according to Žižek is like a cannibal who takes, "the fantasmatic stuff of the I" and swallows it. He argues that *The Silence of the Lambs* illustrates the situation of analysis. "The analysand confesses to the analyst, the kernel of her being, her fundamental fantasy, (the crying of the lambs) Hannibal Lecter," according to Žižek "is not cruel enough to be a Lacanian analyst, since in psychoanalysis we must pay the analyst so that they will allow us to offer them our Dasein on a plate."[32]

This cannibalism of the master was played out throughout Tito's Yugoslavia where so many Slovenians, Croatians, and Serbians were executed; their only crime: they were not communists. It is perhaps no mere accident that Žižek turns to Lacan, the psychoanalytic tyrant to find a Master worthy to eat his *objet a* much like the Italian fascists who devoured all the cats they could find in Dalmatia and Hercegovina to keep themselves from starving.

Žižek is wrong to argue that "reality is never given in its totality; there is always a void, gaping in the midst, filled out by monstrous apparitions."[33] This may be the case with Hitchcock films, Magritte's paintings or Grimm's fairy tales. These examples are fictions and like Anakin failing to kill the Sith Lord, they do nothing to stop real horror from happening on a daily basis.

I clarify this point with a personal example. When I witnessed the exhumation of corpses from the mass grave near the city of Vukovar that was destroyed by the Yugoslavian and Serbian Army, what I saw was not an

32. Ibid., 148.
33. Žižek, *Tarrying With the Negative*, 105.

objet petit-à but the noumenon itself. While Žižek wants to place belief in a "fantasmatic core inaccessible to my conscious experience"[34] this core is already present in conscious experience. It is already within my life-world. It makes itself seen even as I attempt to tear out my eyes.

Traditionally communist societies have allowed the private distillation of alcohol. A drunken public are like dead poets. Lacan teaches us to enjoy. A proper defiance must be sober. Imaginary enjoyment only increases our docility. I think here of shows like *NipTuck* where fantasy is sold to desperate housewives and frozen TV dinner eaters. Watching the Imaginary that the Symbolic authority has prepared for us only entraps us in more of the same.

Žižek's answer to achieve liberation is "to demand from the master that he acts as one."[35] Žižek is wrong here. To treat the master as master as Žižek suggest is to repeat Plato's mistake that supported tyrants and Heidegger's mistake that supported National Socialism.

Is not Žižek acting like the hero from the film Borat who during a dinner party asks where the toilet is and returns with his excrement in plastic bag, asking the hostess where he should put it. The act of resistance here is to refuse the shit-of-the-other and to say that I see through the civil-lies of your ideology.

While American, British and European leftists were being dined by Tito, his torture chambers were full of those who did resist the stupidity of the Master's Discourse. Those who told the Master that his "bait" was suspect found the base from which they became free. This base, contra Marx is not economic but ethical.

34. Žižek, *Interrogating the Real*, 93.
35. de Sutter, ed., *Žižek and the Law*, 227.

3

The Para-Exlax View

On their great grave-highway did I seat myself, and even beside
the carrion and vultures.

—Nietzsche, *Thus Spoke Zarathustra*, "Of Old and New Tablets"

The Parallax View has been described as Žižek's *magnum opus*. I will
argue that Žižek continues his obfuscation by attempting to rehabilitate the
philosophy of dialectical materialism from a Hegelian-Lacanian point of
view. In this text, Žižek continues with his embrace of "revolutionary terror"
as he attempts to locate, "the gap between humanity and its own inhuman
excess."[1] While Žižek clearly brings out his opposition to the "usual gang of
democracy-to-come deconstructionists-post-secular Levinasian-respect-
for-otherness-suspects," he warns that "a number of cruel traps have been
set" for these Levinasian Derrideans.[2]

Žižek asserts "our vision of reality is anamorphically distorted."[3] Direct
access to the thing is possible. The only thing that prevents direct access is
excessive theorizing. Žižek claims that the real is "the thing which eludes
our grasp and the distorting screen which makes us missing the Thing."[4]
Perhaps this holds for a disciple of Lacan but others are not limited by the
gap that Žižek constructs.

1. Žižek, *The Parallax View*, 5.
2. Ibid., 11.
3. Žižek, *In Defense of Lost Causes*, 288.
4. Žižek, *Less Than Nothing*, 535.

While Žižek criticizes postmodernism for its relativism, it is clear that the only relativism is in the hegemonic theorizing that Žižek engages in which cuts off the dignity of the person. It appears that Žižek has not read Lacan very closely. Žižek, to use Lacan's words, "has become all of a sudden mad about a truth, about the first pretty face encountered at the first turn in the road."[5] Žižek wants to return to a master signifier but Lacan declares, "What is striking, and what no one seems to see is that from that moment on . . . the master signifier only appears ever more unassailable, precisely in its impossibility. Where is it? How can it be named? Other than through its murderous effect of course."[6] The question is how do we move away from the tolerable exploitation of liberalism and at the same time bury the intolerable exploitation of communism?

What Žižek does is teach us how to desire, as if the structural lack/void could be filled by Hegel's collected works. The truth of the situation is that the regimes that Žižek supports attempted to fill the void with murdered bodies. This is what Žižek refers to as "the frenzy of revolutionary upheaval." I cannot help recalling here the scene from *Aliens* when Sigourney Weaver's character is trapped in the infirmary by the scientist who turns off the camera so that the marines cannot hear or see her calls for help. The scientist was attempting to give birth to the inhuman. While Žižek often praises the inhuman in opposition to "the human all too human" atrocities, it is precisely humanity that must be defended.

Žižek continues with his critique of Levinas for having a "too narrow definition of what is human."[7] According to Žižek what Levinas misses is "the paradox that every normative determination of the 'human' is possible only against an impenetrable ground of 'inhuman.'"[8] Basically Levinas has not incorporated Lacan's insights even though he has experienced the inhuman himself. Žižek who knows better states, "this is not how a survivor of the Shoah, how one who actually experience the ethical abyss of the Shoah, thinks and writes. This is how those who feel guilty for observing the catastrophe from a minimal safe distance think."[9]

Again, Žižek is describing his own lack of judgment. He is thinking about danger from his apartment in Ljubljana, holding session on the evils

5. Lacan, OSP, 172.
6. Lacan, OSP, 178.
7. Žižek, *The Parallax View*, 111.
8. Ibid.
9. Žižek, Santner, and Reinhard, *The Neighbor*, 160.

of capitalism while his royalties from all his books keep pouring in. Who is being fooled here?

Žižek's incorrect observations should be supplemented with his own experience when Slovenia was attacked by the defacto Serbian Army. He was at a maximum safe distance, reading Lacan while his city burned.[10]

Žižek relies on works of fiction to theorize about reality. Do we really learn how to sacrifice our freedom by watching *3:10 to Yuma*? The works that Žižek chooses and the films that he reviews confront us with interpretative dilemmas that avoid doing anything about the ideological predicaments that we are mired in.

When Žižek claims that "no material property distinguishes Duchamp's urinal from the urinal in a nearby public lavatory,"[11] he is again mistaken. What distinguishes the one from the other is that one is signed R. Mutt and does not contain any material substance, while the other is urine stained and filled with discarded chewing gum.

Duchamp's readymade bicycle wheel on a stool is precisely intended as a description of Žižek's project. The Lacanian-Leninist wheel fixed on a stool goes nowhere. It spins and repeats its gestures believing that it has travelled great distances.

Žižek's philosophy cannot think the person. This is why he can write, "it was only Soviet Communism which despite, the catastrophe, it stands for dispossess true inner greatness . . . if we really want to name an act which was truly daring, for which one truly had to 'have the balls' to try the impossible, but which was simultaneously a horrible act, an act causing suffering beyond comprehension, it was Stalin's forced collectivization in the Soviet Union at the end of the 1920's."[12] There is really nothing more to say here. It is quite perverse to bring Kierkegaard to the rescue by claiming that such violence was a "work of love."

Žižek discerns in these acts, "a ruthless but sincere and enthusiastic will toward a total revolutionary upheaval of the social body to create a new state, intelligentsia, legal systems."[13] Of course, since Žižek's parents were

---

10. See Bijelić, "An Introduction," 701–7. Bijelić alerts us to "the discrepancy between Žižek's declared leftist politics and his neoliberal practice which after cancelling each other out amounts to "empty talk" (703). The best critique that I have heard thus far is that Žižek is "selling us an air guitar."

11. Žižek, ed., *Lacan*, 221.

12. Žižek, *The Parallax View*, 285

13. Ibid.

communists he was never on the receiving end of ruthless and enthusiastic Stalinist "love"

When Žižek writes, "Stalinism still conceived itself as part of the Enlightenment tradition within which truth is accessible to any rational man."[14] How can Žižek speak here of truth when Stalinist show trials were built on falsity and deception and killing "criminals" for crimes they did not commit?

Žižek continues with his Stalinist Love by claiming that prisoners in the Gulag actually sent Stalin telegrams wishing him all the best. For Žižek, this shows that "Stalinism did not sever the last thread that linked it to civilization. The lowest gulag inmate still participated in universal reason. He had access to the Truth of History."[15] Does Žižek really believe this? I would like to test his theory out. He could always become an inmate in North Korea, China, or Cuba to see if he as an inmate "still participated in universal reason."

For Žižek, the tragedy of the October Revolution was that it not achieves its "unique emancipatory potential." He has little to say about its Stalinist outcome. Žižek promotes communism but only for others. In this regard he resembles Stalin and the current rulers of China who want others to follow communism when they themselves remain steadfast capitalists. Žižek is the ultimate capitalist who deserves the Thales' Olive Press award. He performs the exact opposite of what he recommends in his writings. He is like Levinas who talks about the face of the other while denying the Palestinians a face. Indeed, if there is no big Other, then the universalism that Žižek upholds at the expense of the singular person makes no sense. His support of Badiou's thesis that "we should reinvent emancipatory terror today" is not a profound insight. It is a murderous insight aimed at eliminating personhood.

Žižek's program changes nothing because in his own words, "Better to do nothing than to engage in localized acts whose ultimate function is to make the system run more smoothly."[16] It is for this reason that Žižek prefers the politics of Bartelby who says, "I would prefer not to." This is not an act that will change the co-ordinates of our reality.

The revolutions that Žižek favors are excessive. They had an excessive love of murder. The question to ask here is: Why have so many followed

14. Ibid., 289.

15. Ibid., 291.

16. Žižek, *The Universal Exception*, 221.

this Lacanian film scholar who by all accounts has read Lacan and Derrida badly as if he were a great philosopher and revolutionary? What are his believers and followers hoping to accomplish by taking a Lacanian framework and placing it over the world? This interface allows for the dominance of the imaginary. This is why Žižek is fond of interpreting cartoons.

In reading Žižek I have realized that "the game is up." To cite Žižek and return his words back to him, "is it not true that when a political system is in deep crisis, it drags on only because it doesn't notice that it is already dead."[17] Žižek's work while hailed as radical "is out of sync with the actual state of things."[18] Again, what he says about Ted Hughes Birthday Letters "with their fake mythologizing" turning it "into an ethically repulsive text"[19] is precisely how Žižek's work should be read.

17. Žižek, *The Parallax View,* 201.
18. Ibid.
19. Ibid., 203.

4

Ninja Castration

And with fifty mirrors around you, which flattered your play of colours, and repeated it!

—Nietzsche, *Thus Spoke Zarathustra*, "The Land of Culture"

IN *FIRST AS TRAGEDY, Then as Farce*, Žižek tell us that the title is intended as "an elementary IQ test for the reader."[1] Žižek contends that if the reader sees twentieth century totalitarianism as a tragedy and the call to return to communism as a farce then "the book should be forcibly confiscated."[2] The tragedy that Žižek has in mind is the attacks of September 11 and the farce refers to the financial meltdown of 2008. If we define tragedy as the unforeseen then neither totalitarianism nor 9/11 qualifies as tragedy. Both events were clearly foreseen. The only farce would be what Žižek vehemently defends, namely, communism and its death pit gulags.

Žižek is against the "preachers and practitioners" of liberal democracy. He repeats his mantra inversion that we only image we believe in our beliefs and in spite of this "imaginary distance" we continue to uphold and practice in what do not actually believe. Isn't it the other way around? The practitioners and preachers of communism didn't actually believe in their new world order. They invented a farce that resulted in the greatest number of individuals killed by one ideology. On the surface these preachers talked

1. Žižek, *First as Tragedy, Then as Farce*, 1.
2. Ibid.

about socialism but practiced capitalism. The communist leaders accumulated their wealth from the very classes they sought to liberate.

Žižek cites the conditions of the rich in Sao Paulo, Brazil which "boasts 250 heliports in its central downtown area." Žižek believes that the rich of Sao Paulo are "insulating themselves from the dangers of mingling with ordinary people."[3] The rich choose helicopter travel for the same reason communist dignitaries chose armoured limousine travel; they are fearful of being kidnapped, tortured, and having their ears cut off. The heliports have little to do with films like *Blade Runner* or *Fifth Element* where according to Žižek, "ordinary people swarming through the dangerous streets down below, whilst the rich float around on a higher level, up in the airs."[4]

I contend that Žižek's "diagnosis of our predicament" is the repetition of a Lacanian farce and his goal of locating "aspects of our situation which opens the space for new forms of communist praxis"[5] should be fought against.

Žižek's repetitions cannot offer us anything new. We have tasted this gulag bread before. Žižek is free to take the side of communism as I am equally free to oppose its effects. It is clear that the idea of communism can no longer be used as a tool, as a fulcrum from which to change our co-ordinates. Žižek urges communism to be "re-invented in each new historical situation."[6] Such a repetition will only be paved with new corpses. Žižek is no longer convincing because what he defends has already shown itself to be a broken ideology.

Žižek calls for a stealthy castration of those in power. He writes, "The task is not to conduct the castration in a direct climactic confrontation, but to undermine those in power with patient ideological critical work so that although they are still in power, one all of a sudden notices that the powers-the-be are afflicted with unnaturally high-pitched voices."[7] Žižek does not want a direct confrontation. He proceeds like a ninja sniper. To act "in full fidelity to the communist idea," means to enact terror, famine and genocide.

Can there be forgiveness for those who supported the communist idea? Žižek urges a return to the core, to the kernel of what communism

3. Ibid., 5.
4. Ibid., 5.
5. Ibid.
6. Ibid., 6.
7. Ibid., 7.

means. But this kernel is already diseased. The documentary *Mao: A Chinese Tale* shows us why Žižek's solution must be trashed. One historian estimates that 38 million Chinese died in Mao's Great Leap Forward. During this time cannibalism saved many from starvation. Those alive feared the living because they might be eaten. How ironic those private plots of lands saved some Chinese from famine while forced collectivization lead to unspeakable suffering. Žižek's embrace of communism is a return to more of the same.

When he speaks of the tyranny of the market and uses Lacanian ideas to show how domination functions, one has no other recourse but to yawn. The spirit of Žižek's "vast erudition" has ended up as a bone in the throat of those who refuse to think for themselves. This is why I am not stunned by "Žižek's sheer intelligence" nor am I impressed by his endless creativity in reading in reading both the philosophical tradition and popular culture through Lacanian lenses.

The truth of the matter is that Lacanian concepts laid to rest by psychoanalysts have been resurrected by English professors and literary theorists. If Lacan's theories by all accounts were detrimental from a therapeutic standpoint they would be even more stupid if they were used to analyze the symptoms of our time.

For all this alleged engagement with high theory, Žižek merely exposes the inadequacy of his own position. The reduction of the globe to a Leninist-Marxist colony with Lacanianism as the Master Discourse is Žižek's own fantasy where he "knows very well how things are" but still acts as if he does not.

Žižek's nihilism that asserts the "pure void of negativity"[8] cannot offer us any ground from which to transform our life-world. When Travis in *Taxi Driver* clears "the blood and cum" from the back seat of his cab he is not allowing the other to experience pleasure for him. *Taxi Driver* shows us that the porn theatre is no different from the campaign office.

Žižek has his supporters. Paul Taylor argues that Žižek provides an "inimitable blend of provocation and deep insights."[9] Taylor sees method in Žižek's madness. Jodi Dean argues that "Žižek's work is indispensable to any effort to break out of the present political impasses."[10] Dean contends, "as long as we refuse to draw a line in the sand and say enough is

8. Ibid., 56.
9. Taylor, "Why Žižek Now?," 1.
10. Dean, "Why Žižek," 18–32.

enough, the right will continue its exploitation and repression of the world's people."[11] Somehow Žižek is supposed to help the free the oppressed of the world with his notion of "enjoyment as the being-there of the subject."[12]

Dean and Taylor would be better served if they went to the Third World and dug a well rather than peddle Žižek as a solution to oppression. In fact, Žižek could help the oppressed if he actually took a portion of the sales of his books and went to provide clean water to an African village rather than speculated "about the ideological ramifications of the structure of toilets."[13] Dean lauds Žižek's claim that "the brutal violence of Stalinism testifies to the authenticity of the Russian revolution"[14] is not shock art. The Derridean lesson is clear: Beware of Lacanian proletariats with tenure who want to liberate you into year zero.

It is difficult to understand why Žižek is critical of Western Buddhism for enabling "you to fully participate in the frantic capitalist game while sustaining the perception that you are not really in it."[15] Isn't this what Žižek is doing? The fetish for the Buddhists is the doctrine of no permanent self or in Lacanese there is only pure void. What values is Žižek saving here, other than his own inverted assessments that fill graduate students with awe and wonder?

The truth of the Communist revolution lies in the 100 million murdered bodies. They are proof enough for me that there is no radical emancipatory project within communism. Žižek is fond of citing Beckett's phrase, "fail again, fail better," as if to say that the left needs another 80 million corpses before it can be successful. Žižek has no moral or theoretical authority to complain about new walls and slums when the system he glorifies excelled in creating such grand architecture.

Žižek wishes to "participate in the universal space of the community of believers."[16] It is clear that the graduate students who hear him speak and the tenured leftist professors who are so oppressed will not be setting up barricades and throwing Molotov cocktails at the capitalistic police. Fanon is

11. Ibid., 19.

12. Ibid., 26.

13. McGowan, "Serious Theory," 56–67.

14. See Parker, Review of Žižek's Politics, 89.

15. Žižek, First as Tragedy, Then as Farce, 66.

16. Ibid., 106.

correct when he writes, "I find myself in the world and I recognize that I have one right alone: that of demanding human behavior from the other."[17]

What are the consequences to be drawn from Žižek's analysis? Stalin and Lenin must be resurrected so that those like Berlusconi can be overthrown. Liberal freedom is to be replaced with "disciplinary terror."[18] Žižek has no difficulties as he recommends enforcing this new world order. Žižek closes his book with the invitation, "You've had your anti-communist fun, and you are pardoned for it, time to get serious once again."[19]

Before we run back to the Communist Homestead after our capitalist *Rumspringa* we need to ask if Žižek really expects his words to ignite a revolution. Žižek contends, "there is definitely something terrifying about this attitude-however, this terror is nothing less than the condition of freedom."[20]

One can critique capitalism and all its ills without leaping into the loving arms of Lenin's refrigerated corpse. Recall how corporate sponsors abandoned Tiger Woods after revelations of his infidelity surfaced on the green. I suppose that the Lacanian lesson is that the superstar golfer is free to play eighteen holes and sink his balls under the adulation of his public but when he ventures into the private realm his balls must stay in faithful repose. What does golf have to do with fidelity? The same thing Žižek has to do with philosophy and inciting revolutions: Nothing at all.

Do corporations really invest in the capital of public stupidity so that the image of a golfer as husband, family man, and exemplary citizen must be upheld so that the maximum amount of razors, shoes, and energy drinks can be sold? Was Tiger not being Lacanian by following his desire where it led him? Why should corporations care what he does in private? Are they acting from a sense of moral authority or plain optics? The toilet paper executive who does nothing and earns a profit while others do all the work is the essence of capital. Knowing this does not make me run to North Korea to sing a birthday song to the "great leader."

17. Fanon, *Black Skin, White Mask*.

18. Žižek, *First as Tragedy, Then as Farce*, 125.

19. Ibid., 157.

20. Žižek, *Mao Tse Tung*, 28.

5

Mirages in the Desert of the Real

The greatest events—are not our noisiest, but our stillest hours.
Not around the inventors of new noise, but around the inventors
of new values, does the world revolve; inaudibly it revolves.

—Nietzsche, *Thus Spoke Zarathustra*, "Of Great Events"

IN WELCOME TO THE *Desert of the Real: Five Essays on September 11 and
related Dates*. Žižek offers his philosophical understanding of 9/11. He concludes his analysis with the insight that we must avoid the temptation of the
either/or. The real problem for Žižek is democracy as it is being presented
to us. There may be other alternatives to fundamentalism other than the
political system of liberal democracy.

Žižek tells us nothing new. He insists that global capitalism is in fact
fundamentalist and the U.S. government was the catalyst for the rise of
Islamic radicals. While critical of the current state of affairs, Žižek never
concretely spells out his alternative, other than to offer us Hegel, Marx,
Lenin, and Lacan as ideological saviors, who may make our desert existence bearable.

To help explain our current predicament, Žižek cites the red ink joke: "A
guy was sent from East Germany to work in Siberia. He knew his mail would
be read by censors, so he told his friends: 'Let's establish a code. If a letter you
get from me is written in blue ink, it is true what I say. If it is written in red
ink, it is false.' After a month, his friends get the first letter. Everything is in
blue. It says, this letter: 'Everything is wonderful here. Stores are full of good

food. Movie theatres show good films from the west. Apartments are large and luxurious. The only thing you cannot buy is red ink.'"[1]

Žižek's conclusion is as follows: "[W]e feel free because we lack the very language to articulate our unfreedom. What this lack of red ink means is that today, all the main terms we use to designate the present conflict—'war on terrorism,' 'democracy and freedom,' 'human rights' and so on—are false terms."[2]

Notice the conditions under which Žižek writes these observations. While claiming that liberal democracy has "refined" conditions of censorship, he is clearly free to think and write what he wishes. The only thing that Žižek fails to reveal is whether he writes with red or blue ink and which ink is out of stock. The question becomes complicated when one uses a lap-top to protect the legacy of Lenin, Stalin, and Mao. If one traces Žižek's production during the time of Yugoslav Communism, it becomes clear that he did not write, "there must be an alternative to the Yugoslav system which murdered an estimated one million Croatians, not to mention all the Slovenians, Serbians and Bosnians."

Simply put, Žižek is posing as a critic of liberal democracy while collecting his paycheck every month. This much like the American Marxists still writing about class struggle, Althusser and Mao from their Ivy League tenured fortresses. My point here is that Žižek had many opportunities to create an event, to give birth to a defining ethical act, but he did not.

Žižek asks the question concerning "today's fundamentalist terror" Is not its goal, he asks, "to awaken us, Western citizens, from our numbness, from immersion in our everyday ideological universes."[3]

The goal of fundamentalist terror is not to "awaken" us from our "numbness" and "immersion." Its goal is the destruction of those who do not believe in the supremacy of its system. The fundamentalist terror is not like the cutters—people who cut themselves with razors to feel alive. Žižek believes, "cutting is a radical attempt to (re)gain a hold on reality."[4] Is this a solution to get us out of our liberal ideological numbness? Žižek's maxim seems to be that cutting oneself is good because it makes us feel alive. Fundamentalist terror is good for Žižek, because it allows for the establishment

1. Žižek, *Welcome to the Desert of the Real*, 1.
2. Ibid.
3. Ibid., 9.
4. Ibid., 10.

of an anti-capitalist order. Beating oneself up, pace *Fight Club*, is good because it helps to bring down the capitalist order.

Žižek wants us to experience the real horror of existence rather than its semblance. But he safeguards himself from the horror that he wants others to experience. This is why he says that during the early 1990s when he was considered for a government post in the Slovenian government, "the only one which interested me was that of the Minister of the Interior or head of the secret service."[5] Given Heidegger's great mistake as rector, we can only imagine how repressive Slovenian society would have become if Žižek was head of the secret service. All two million Slovenians would be subject to Lacanian analysis, producing the world's first Lacanian state.

Taking Freud's insight that dreams are wish fulfilments, it is easy to criticize Žižek's hard core insights. Take the following typical Žižekian observation. He writes, "Is not the ultimate figure of passion for the Real the option we get on hard-core websites to observe the inside of a vagina from the vantage point of a tiny camera at the top of the penetrating dildo . . . when we get too close to the desired object, erotic fascination turns into disgust at the Real of bare flesh."[6]

I take this as an apt description of Žižek's method of analysis. Lacan of course is the "penetrating dildo"; the mechanical phallus charged up with Hegelian re-chargeable *aufhebung* batteries. Žižek's analysis is provided by the tiny camera on top. Because he is so close to his object of desire, he fails to see the big picture. Here he is like the hero in the film *Kingsman: Secret Service* claiming his reward.

Žižek argues that we should be liberated from our fantasies so that we can "confront reality as it really is."[7] So that while "poor people dream of becoming American, Americans dream about global catastrophes."[8] Did Americans not confront reality as it is on 9/11 or did the passengers confront the Real as played out by the fantasy space of the Saudi hijackers? The ethical insight here would be not to ride on the Other's fantasy but to face the real like St. Francis's encounter with the leper.

In his *Treatise on Human Nature* Schelling makes a distinction between existence and insistence. Schelling shows how that which no longer exists can continue to insist. This is a classic definition of both guilt and

5. Ibid., 6.
6. Ibid.
7. Ibid., 17.
8. Ibid., 19.

mourning. The question remains how does one redeem an act so that the non-existence of what I should have done, no longer haunts my space? Given that what is done always already generates its own excess (the principle of dissemination) we can never be certain of the final outcome. Not even "God" can predict all possibilities. Is it simply the case that radical Evil is the excess that arises out good intentions? The Thing cannot be reduced to such Lacanian simplicity. If "power generates its own excess" as Žižek claims, then such power is not enlightened. Žižek tries to explain: "Is not the truth behind the fact that Bin Laden and the Taliban emerged as part of the CIA supported anti-Soviet guerilla movement in Afghanistan and behind the fact that Noriega in Panama was an ex-CIA agent? Is not the USA fighting its own excess in all these cases?"[9]

Is it simply the case here that the Taliban are fighting against their primordial father, Uncle Sam within the horizon of his apocalypse now? Arguing that the Taliban are the excess of US power ignores the excess within the Taliban itself. Does Žižek apply his arguments of power/excess to Slovenia's declaration of Independence from the Yugoslav Communist Federation? Would this declaration be seen as the excess of Yugoslav central power whereby the Yugoslav Army had no choice but to act against the excessive clause in the 1974 Constitution that guaranteed the right of the Republics to self-determination? The point here is that Žižek just keeps up appearances without going to the end to actually confront the Real. This is why I read Žižek's authorship as a series of unsuccessful spasms incapable of obtaining full satisfaction.

Žižek wants to argue that "in past centuries Islam has been significantly more tolerant toward other religions than Christianity. Now is also the time to remember that it was through the Arabs that in the Middle Ages, we in Western Europe regained access to our Ancient Greek heritage."[10]

There is much to say about Žižek's one-sided analysis here. The phrase "significantly more tolerant" cannot erase the many acts of horror that the Ottoman Empire inflicted on the Croatian Catholic population in Bosnia-Hercegovina. Five hundred years of oppression is hardly an exercise in tolerance. Of course, it makes sense for a Slovenian to talk about Islamic tolerance when Croatian, Bosnia-Hercegovina, and Serbia lived through the tremors of Ottoman "tolerance."

9. Ibid., 27.
10. Ibid., 41.

Žižek's thesis that we are "in effect dealing with a clash of fundamentalisms"[11] is simplistic. Can it be that Žižek has forgotten the element of justice? Once, about two hundred years ago, an Ottoman pasha was riding his horse through my family's land in Hercegovina. He decided to allow his horse to feed in our wheat field. My great-great-great-grandmother concluded that the Pasha was depriving her family of nourishment; wheat being a necessary staple. My grandmother did what justice demanded. She gave the pasha a good thrashing tied him on his horse and sent him back to Mostar in good cowboy fashion. While focused on great events, Žižek remains a movie metanarrative theoretician unable, as Kierkegaard would say, to focus on the single individual.

Žižek's criticism of current politics is that the Left misses today's political dimension as the right acts out its capitalist fantasies. Žižek writes, "The first duty of a progressive intellectual (if this term has any meaning left in it today) is not fight the enemy's struggles for him."[12] Whose struggle is Žižek waging? Kant's great insight in *What is Enlightenment?* is that Masters will tell you that you cannot do anything without them so that they may enjoy their privileged status.

I agree with Žižek when he writes that we cannot buy into Spielberg's views in *The Land Before Time* where the small dinosaurs have to find a place for the bigger dinosaurs who are "louder and they're stronger and they make a bigger fuss, but way down deep inside, I think they're kids like us."[13] This cartoon wisdom fails to educate. It merely trains. Cartoons are a child's first exposure to state propaganda and it teaches a lesson of lies. It is not a *Little Bear* world where Molly and her dolly walk over to grandma's house watching Diego with his magic vest run with the jaguars while Dora does the a*ufhebung* stomp through the forest to arrive at her indifferent parent's house unharmed.

Citing the famous words of Christ that he came to bring the sword and division out of love for humanity, Žižek writes, "When somebody kills just one true enemy of humanity, he (not kills, but) saves the whole of humanity. The true ethical test is not only the readiness to save victims but also—even more perhaps—the ruthless dedication to annihilating those who made them victims."[14]

11. Ibid., 32.
12. Ibid., 55.
13. Ibid., 65.
14. Ibid., 68.

So when Christ says on the one hand that he brings the sword and on the other that those who live by the sword, die by the sword, was he not predicting his own sword-caused death? The problem here of course is that Žižek believes that Stalin, Lenin, and Mao were Christ-like as they brought the sword. What is required is that we fight against such absurdity that poses as great truth. It is like Putin who invades Ukraine and then declares that the United States plan to launch airstrikes in Syria against ISIL positions is "a violation of International law." The truth-effect emerges at the very point where it is supressed by unthinking adulation. Žižek's thought is a preface that greets us at the gulag entrance.

The season five opening episode of the *Walking Dead* entitled, "No Sanctuary" holds a clear answer to Žižek and Badiou and their supporters who urge us to return to Communism. The episode provides a clear example of how communism always leads to terror. Recall that Rick and the group are making their way to a sanctuary called Terminus where all will be welcome. The signs point to a safe haven that will provide rest, peace and sanctuary. Terminus is full of well-armed cannibals. The outwardly charitable and social minded Terminians are really sadistic people-eaters and butchers.

As Rick's group makes their way into the shelter they are disarmed and taken to a train-car where they will be processed. While in the car they make weapons using scraps stripped from their clothes and the car's interior. Their cannibals release tear gas into the car, catching them off guard. Rick's group is brought to a human slaughterhouse, where Terminus residents begin bludgeoning them with baseball bats and slitting their throats. Two are slaughtered in this manner before the Terminus leader Gareth interrupts to interrogate Rick.

As the interrogation continues, Carol who is smeared with walker's blood discovers the Terminus shrine and its gate-keeper Mary. Mary explains, "You're the butcher or you're the cattle." Carol shoots her in the leg and leaves her to be devoured by walkers. Mary's answer summarizes the history of Communist terror. And it is this terror that Žižek, Badiou, and their supporters wish us to return to.

The ethical lesson here is never to trust those who promise us sanctuary when they are cannibals in disguise. Lenin, Stalin, Mao, Pol Pot, and their ilk were never interested in socialism and the greater good of humanity. They were first and foremost butchers who were allowed to kill with impunity. The fact that Žižek is exalted as a high ranking philosopher and theorist when he applauds these individuals is simply mind-boggling. To follow their philosophy is to walk into the slaughterhouse where human bodies hang.

6

Ethics without Paradox

It is the stillest words which bring the storm. Thoughts that come with doves' footsteps guide the world.

—Nietzsche, *Thus Spoke Zarathustra*, "The Stillest Hour"

In *Democracy Matters: Winning the Fight Against Imperialism*, Cornel West spells out the ills that are plaguing American society. The ills according to West are "free-market fundamentalism that results in a corporate-dominated political economy where business leaders with wealth and power take the place of genuine democratic leadership."[1] In addition to free market fundamentalism West believes that another ill is "aggressive militarism that sacrifices working class youth of color."[2] The American system according to West strips away liberty in favor of security. To combat these strains of anti-democratic behavior West urges a return to the Socratic legacy of questioning, the Jewish prophetic commitment to Justice intertwined with the lessons of blues music and jazz. West writes, "We desperately need the deep democratic energy of this Socratic questioning in these times of rampant sophistry on the part of our political elites and their media pundits . . . in the face of callous indifference to the suffering wrought by our imperialism we must draw on the prophetic."[3]

1. West, *Democracy Matters*, 3.
2. Ibid., 5.
3. Ibid., 17.

West sees the essence of the blues as allowing us "to stare painful truths in the face" in order to persevere "without cynicism or pessimism."[4] West is eloquent and I sympathize with his ethical stance but his text shows how intellectuals are losing the struggle. Socratic questioning, the prophetic call to justice, and tragicomic hope always arrive late on the scene. The corpses are in full view or have been buried. It is too late to question and too late to play an E minor chord when the forces of oppression and dehumanization have completed their work.

Do we require two thousand more years to realize that Socratic questioning is short-sighted? We require different tools to combat imperialism, capitalist excess, communist oppression, and corporate greed. While our songs record painful details and brutal experiences our "righteous indignation."[5] is not enough.

It is not enough to play blues on our iPod while reading downloaded versions of Cervantes, Chekhov, and Pynchon all the while complaining about "oppression". The Derridean question is how to awaken the "democracy-to-come" in a world that is sedated with comforting illusions?

How to take the "country back from the hands of corrupted plutocratic and imperial elites,"[6] is a question that Socratic questioning cannot answer. Indeed, Socrates allowed himself to be murdered by "corrupted plutocratic and imperial elites." As such, Socrates has nothing to offer us but a trip to prison. This is the Socratic legacy that we have inherited from the Greeks.

Is the solution to become a corporate elite so that we too can control market forces for our own benefit? Should we all become oil and gas executives who raise prices whenever they wish while telling us that "the market dictates the price" or do we short circuit the market with a *Fight Club* knock-out? Believing in democratic principles and actually implementing them requires more than piercing our noses, tattooing ourselves with pirate symbols, and riding our skateboards to Wall Street to throw stones with the grandfathers of *Mai 68*.

According to West, the current political system is based on "mendacity, manipulation and misinformation."[7] West does not spell out how to found a political system based on "truth, integrity and principles."[8] When-

---

4. Ibid., 21.
5. Ibid., 19.
6. Ibid., 23.
7. Ibid., 28.
8. Ibid., 28.

ever I hear American philosophers speak like this I wonder if they have ever heard of Canada? I may be biased here but there are good reasons that theorists like Henry Giroux left the States to live in Canada.

Nihilism is not the culprit here. Those who West labels as nihilists actually do believe. They are full of belief. From Evangelical preachers who keep crucifying Jesus while sending out little packets of miracle water for five dollars, to corporate bankers who charge $1.50 for ATM "service fees" the belief in the power of dollar (The God we trust) is the gospel. The belief in the bottom line is not nihilism. The prophetic cry in the wilderness, "Look at what is being done!" bounces back as "Yes it is being done," and resounds with Žižek's "And where is the judgment?" The "free and frank press"[9] speaks the truth about our society but as West notes without being aware "of their own complicity in superficiality and simplistic reportage."[10] For example, while I was writing this, broadcasting was interrupted to tell us that Teddy Kennedy was being released from the hospital after having been diagnosed with a brain tumor. The media did not report, at the same time, how many Americans are without health care or are unable to get chemo-therapy. The American market eats its own. West points out the paradox of Thomas Jefferson, revolutionary freedom fighter against the British and "a cowardly aristocratic slaveholder of hundreds of Africans in his beloved Virginia."[11] The Declaration of Independence has turned into an imperialist document especially in the genocidal treatment of indigenous peoples and those forced into slavery. Democracy as a way of being has never really existed. Liberated from one tyranny, America went on to enslave other cultures.

For me the truth of Socrates is clear. Why turn to Socrates as an ideal when he abandoned his family? Why turn to Marxism as an ideal when the truth of Marx was visible in the manner in which he allowed his wife and children to suffer? Applying these insights to Žižek's work we see that he participates in the very mode of that which he criticizes.[12] This does not prevent theorists like Jodi Dean and Adrian Johnston from exalting Žižek's work.

Jodi Dean's *Žižek's Politics* outlines Žižek's universalist stance and his refusal to accept democracy as the ultimate political horizon. Dean argues

9. Ibid., 39.

10. Ibid.

11. Ibid., 43.

12. Žižek, "Cultural Studies versus the 'Third Culture,'" 30.

that Žižek provides a radical reformulation of the most pressing problems of our time. Simply put, the combination that Žižek's puts together—a mixture of psychoanalysis and Hegel—makes Žižek's work fall short of effecting any change. Dean argues that Žižek "presents a systematic theory of politics. The key component of this system is the category of enjoyment.[13] The Lacanian notion of enjoyment "denotes an intense excessive, pleasure-pain." To believe this is to believe the person who says, "I am beating you for your own good."

According to Dean, "Žižek challenges us to recognize and take responsibility for our own enjoyment."[14] For Dean, this means to be aware of what we do, "in practices and behaviors in which we *persist* even as we know better."[15] To know X and to do Y is an act of stupidity. I know that reading *Women's World* will not solve my food addiction, but I still read the diet and recipe section. If enjoyment is stupid then it cannot lead to any positive political change. The problem with Dean's awe-struck approach is revealed in her own words. She writes, "I do not debate Žižek's interpretation of other philosophers."[16] This is the only way to show that what Žižek presents to his readers is a massive misreading of the philosophical tradition. Žižek's politics of enjoyment strikes me as absurd.

Žižek's excess resembles Alec Baldwin's character in *Glengarry Glen Ross*. Baldwin's character is sent to inspire a down-and-out sales team. He tells the frustrated sellers that they are "pieces of shit". He proceeds to write sales slogans on the board and when asked who he is, he responds with "Fuck you! That's my name." This is how I read Žižek. He shows us his excessive display of enjoyment. But there is no politics to be found in his books. Žižek's fans are captivated and transfixed. The analytics are repulsed, the Lacanians aren't sure what to do, the Marxists like Eagleton praise him for his theoretical insights and dirty jokes. The main question to answer here is why have so many sustained Žižek's fantasy of the "Fuck you" posing as good advice? He is remaining true to his master Lacan. Here are Lacan's words: "For the moment, I am not fucking, I am talking to you. Well! I can have exactly the same satisfaction as if I were fucking. That's what it [sublimation] means. Indeed, it raises the question of whether in fact I am

13. Dean, *Žižek's Politics*, xv.

14. Ibid., xvii.

15. Ibid.

16. Ibid., xx.

not fucking at this moment."[17] If enjoyment is to become a political factor, it must answer how it is possible to be freed from the domination and submission that permeates our lives.

According to Dean, the key feature of Žižek's political theory is "that every ideology relies on an inassimilable kernel of enjoyment."[18] This kernel "can be what we desire but can never achieve . . . it can also be what we want to eliminate but never can."[19] Why should ideology provide us with fullness when we know that it is based on a ruse? Ideology is a "noble lie" to use Plato's words. While Dean argues that Žižek "is trying to clear out a space for radical politics,"[20] I do not see that his "clearing out" of the ideological out-house as radical. For example, when he argues that Stalinism "emerged as the result of a radical emancipatory attempt."[21] The millions murdered under Stalin make his crimes of enjoyment clear. For Žižek, Stalinist ideology, "still exudes an emancipatory potential."[22]

Are we to believe that Stalinism was an aspiration for justice and solidarity when the facts show otherwise? Dean argues that we should read Žižek from the viewpoint of the parallax gap. The parallax gap is "the displacement of an object that comes about when it is viewed from different perspectives."[23] Dean writes, "To see parallax at work stretch your arm out in front of you: point your index finger up: close one eye and then the other while looking at the tip of your finger. Your finger will move back and forth. This movement or shift is parallax."[24]

Here we have great advice on not only how to read Žižek but also on how to change our political systems. The perceptual shift is not a real gap. It is an illusion. The parallax is another distorting screen set up in front of us.

17. Lacan, *Seminar XI: Four Fundamentals of Psychoanalysis*, 197.

18. Dean, *Žižek's Politics*, 47.

19. Ibid.

20. Ibid., 49.

21. Žižek, *Organs without Bodies*, 7.

22. Žižek, *Did Somebody Say Totalitarianism ?*, 133.

23. Dean, *Žižek's Politics*, 52.

24. Ibid.

Take one of Lacan's Mathemes

$$\frac{S_1}{\$}$$

S_1 indicates that the Master is the agent who speaks. $\$$ is the Lacanian split subject which here occupies the position of Truth. Put into plain English: the Master does not speak from the position of Truth. A politics of enjoyment in this case indicates that the Master enjoys or "gets off on" beating others to hide his own weakness. This leads Dean to the grand conclusion, "even the horrifying excess of Stalinist terror testifies to its inner greatness."[25] The purges were "panicky actions and reactions."[26] They "bear witness to the way the revolution involved a real confrontation with class struggle."[27] This is precisely what is wrong with leftist intellectuals—they take the murder of 80 million people and reduce it to "a real confrontation with class struggle." In setting up his four discourses, namely Master, Hysteric, University, and Analyst, Lacan forgot to include the discourse of stupidity posing as high theory. A Father is speaking with his friend. He complains about how fast people drive on the 401 (one of the busiest highways in North America). He cannot understand why some drivers are in a hurry. He gives these great insights while smoking a cigarette next to his newborn son. His moralizing against speed will have disastrous consequence on his son who cannot move. The master desires things to be fixed on one place.

In his *Crossroads in the Labyrinth*, Castoriadis writes, "Any calling into question of the official dogma used to be ruled out as discussion in advance. It needed only to be denounced as coming from the 'class enemy' and therefore as expressing a resistance to the 'class truth' of the proletariat (of which the Party had made itself sole authorized spokesman—just as these psychoanalysts make themselves the sole authorized spokesmen of the "truth of the unconscious' *and* by a logical slip of the theory *of* that truth."[28] Here in a devastating critique, Castoriadis shows how theorists like

---

25. Ibid., 72.
26. Ibid., 79.
27. Ibid., 82.
28. Castoriadis, *Crossroads in the Labyrinth*, 47.

Žižek form a closed circuit that aims to entrap others. This is why Castoriadis calls Lacanianism "a monstrosity"[29]

Castoriadis continues, "the emptiness of this position is concealed behind pseudo-oracular writings, whose aptness for this function is increased by their hermetic character, and by the inability of the disciples to oppose these "algebraic" or "topological" bluffs by any critique, or even by a simple counter-bluff which would be enough to send them up in smoke."[30] Castoriadis is defending the "singular individual" against "parrot-like imitation and 'administrative conformism."[31] According to Castoriadis, the life of the individual is not "a continual voyage around and round the single surface of a Mobius strip, whose possible varieties have been fixed, once and for all, from here to eternity by "structure."[32] He points out that Freud, "strove to think and to render thinkable things which Lacan's theory and practice strive to render unthinkable and impossible."[33]

Castoriadis notes the Franciscan[34] attitude when he critiques Lacan. He writes, "the psyche is radical imagination and, as such it is essentially indeterminacy. Indeterminacy does not mean chaos . . . .the 'universal' is present there under a multitude of forms, as is the knowable; almost everything can be spoken of. But there is, a continual irruption of newness, creation, self-alteration. 'Theory' in the case of most analysts has the function of closing their ears to this newness, this emergence, and to the uniqueness of the subject."[35] This point is missed by Lacan, Žižek, and his followers.

The way out of capitalism is not the enthusiastic embrace of Leninism, Stalinism, and Maoism. It does not involve "resuscitating a revolutionary past to reignite the lost zeal of collective movement against the current conditions of globalization."[36] Nor does it involve accessing the materialist kernel of Christianity. The way out is through a return to the Franciscan notion of haecceity that respects the uniqueness of persons.

29. Ibid., 48.

30. Ibid., 55.

31. Ibid., 59.

32. Ibid., 58.

33. Ibid., 51.

34. One of Tito's first acts when Yugoslavia was formed was to murder the Franciscans in the monastery in Siroki Brijeg, Bosnia-Hercegovina.

35. Castoriadis, *Crossroads in the Labyrinth*, 70.

36. Butler, ed. *The Žižek Dictionary*, 42.

With Žižek and his followers, we are witnessing the "contemporary revival of the most-antiquated sophistry."[37] This sophistry is dangerous because it urges a repeat of the ideologies that have been in-human. What Castoriadis says about Althusser can equally be applied (*mutatis mutandis*)[38] to Žižek: "Althusser, the epoch's symptom in person, found all this wonderfully well suited to the diversionary operations he was carrying out on behalf of the French Communist Party (whose intention was transparent to anyone but an imbecile, was to turn attention away from the monstrosities of Stalinist totalitarianism and its roots in Marxism, as well as from the crisis which it was undergoing) and so, making the sign of Lacan, he took up his place beneath the banner of structuralism."[39] From Stalinism, the Lacanians turned to Maoism in an attempt to make the great leap forward out of the Fifth Arrondissement.

Žižek ensnares those not able to think for themselves. Žižek's great act can never achieve the level of the Act because he can only tell us about the Act through the fiction of films. When Žižek is described as the "Elvis of Cultural Theory" we must agree that he is an entertainer from Slovenia, who took his Lacanian inspired act on the road.

While Althusser argues that "ideology=illusion"[40] This illusion is dangerous for those who do not share the inside joke. Althusser argues that we are "ideological animals by nature." Isn't it the case that we are controlled by ideology. Althusser's impoverished idea of the human as a subject comes from his definition of philosophy as "class struggle in the field of theory." The focus on class forgets the single individual that Kierkegaard and Derrida bring to the forefront of their thought. The class struggle is not the motor of history. It is the gear that has ground down individual persons.

---

37. Castoriadis, *Crossroads in the Labyrinth*, 89.
38. "The necessary changes having been made."
39. Castoriadis, *Crossroads in the Labyrinth*, 108.
40. Althusser, *On Ideology*, 36.

7

The Bread of Lost Causes

That, however, of which I am master and knower, is the brain of
the leech:—that is my world!

—Nietzsche, *Thus Spoke Zarathustra*, "The Leech Gatherer"

IN HIS *DEFENCE OF Lost Causes*, Žižek attempts to counter "the weak
thought" of postmodernism and return to "big explanations," "the violent
imposition of grand solutions." For those of us who have eaten this bread,
Žižek's theoretical formulations are a repetition of exemplary bullshit.
Žižek's leap of faith "in lost causes" is neither a leap of faith nor very faithful. G. K. Chesterton shows why Žižek's "thundering gallop of theory" remains a fun-house ride.[1] For all the pages he has written, Žižek never really
provides a remedy for "the capitalist dynamic." In Chesterton's words, "We
all dislike abject poverty; but it might be another business if we began to
discuss independent and dignified poverty."[2] The causes that Žižek defends
have only filled graves with bodies. It is a fact that his native Slovenia is full
of mass graves—a practical testimony to the Communism that he wishes to
repeat. Žižek's political bargains culled from the trash heap of theory have
nothing to offer, but like all purveyors of junk, his left-overs are filling the
shelves of those who long for the good old days of Soviet terror.

1. Chesterton, *What's Wrong with the World*, v.
2. Chesterton, *Collected Works*, 4:41.

Chesterton argues that "the really courageous man is he who defies tyrannies young as the morning."[3] Žižek has waited until it was safe to write his books. He remains a paper revolutionary who bowed down before the village idiot known as Titoism. Žižek's theorizing is lost and he fails to see the reality of what he is defending. How could he see reality when his theorizing happens within the space of films? The Communist idea has been found wanting. It was tried and it failed. Its legacy is not as unfulfilled as Žižek would make his readers believe. Chesterton writes, "this is the huge modern heresy of altering the human soul to fit its conditions, instead of altering human conditions to fit the soul."[4] All forms of communism attempted to alter what is human to fit its conditions. This Procrustean tactic does not respect the singularity of persons. Žižek's answer appears to be that not everyone has tried out Procruste's bed.

The causes that Žižek defends show an indifference to the individual. But Žižek and Badiou drive ahead to "redeem the emancipatory potential of these failures."[5]

Chesterton writes, "When a crapulous tyranny crushes men down into the dirt, so that their very hair is dirty, the scientific course is clear. It is easier to cut off the hair of the slaves. [. . .] If a house is so built as to knock a man's head off when he enters, it is built wrong."[6] Here it is in straightforward language. The house that Marx devised and that Lenin, Stalin, and Mao built is wrong. It took off heads. But this is Žižek's "fidelity" to the cause. To counter such obscenity, Chesterton defends the single individual. He shows what is obscene in all movements that do not hold the singular person in regard. The point here is that Marx sacrificed his own children and wife for his cause. When Žižek writes, "there are still only two theories which imply and practice such an engaged notion of truth: Marxism and psychoanalysis,"[7] it appears that he has learned little about what truth means.

The film *Songs from the Second Floor*, shows how the bed-pan general fumbles in the dark and rattles the bars of his crib/cage. The youth are sacrificed so that generals can have better pensions. Žižek would know how conscripts in the Yugoslav Army were used to build million dollar villas

3. Ibid., 4:32.

4. Ibid., 4:104.

5. Žižek, *In Defence of Lost Causes*, 8.

6. Chesterton, *Collected Works*, 4:216.

7. Žižek, *In Defence of Lost Causes*, 12.

on Croatia's Adriatic coast for Communist Generals to read *Das Capital* in peace and quiet. With a proper Hegelian inversion one might say, "What better way to house the collected works of Marx, Engels, Lenin, Stalin, Mao, and Tito?" A practice derived from a faulty theory is doomed to failure. It will produce nothing but fault. But Žižek believes that "theory is the theory of a failed practice."[8] And yet, Žižek wants to continue with failure for the sake of theory. Again, failures cannot be redeemed for their emancipatory potential. One does not learn from one's mistakes to make the same mistakes again and again.

Seeing how the Marxist experiment has failed so many times in so many different countries would one more (*encore*) attempt produce a better practice? Who would provide the bail out money to fund Žižek's experiment? I do not accept "the fundamental finitude and limitations of our situation." Neither do I think that Žižek's solution of imposing a Hegelian-Lacanian cage will produce any practical results other than increased book sales for him.

Žižek thinks that the liberal-democratic alternative is "all-too-easy." The struggle for universal emancipation begins with individual emancipation. Žižek would better serve his readers if he were to render problematic his own reliance on totalitarian ideology. Why does he clutch this particular hamster? It is absurd to claim that Stalinism was "a right step in the wrong direction." It was a wrong step from the very beginning, even before it began to crawl. So Žižek seeks, "not to reject terror *in toto* but to reinvent it." [9]He confesses "Stalinism was a nightmare which caused even more human suffering that fascism."[10] But he continues, "this is not the whole truth; there was . . . a redemptive moment which gets lost in the liberal-democratic rejection—and it is crucial to isolate this moment."[11] It is the word "perhaps" that is troublesome here.

How is Žižek actually measuring suffering? Stalinism needs to be rejected *in toto* because its results are evident. The number of corpses it has produced along with the manner in which they were produced, is the clearest evidence of its failure. Stalinism must be rejected not merely out of liberal-democratic sentiment but out of a sense of justice.

8. Ibid., 3.
9. Ibid., 7.
10. Ibid.
11. Ibid.

Žižek claims that the liberal-democratic critique wants to throw out "the dirty war of terror while retaining the pure baby of authentic socialist democracy."[12] The Stalinist waters were always already polluted long before any liberal-democratic critique. Žižek calls for "the full actualization of a Cause, including the inevitable risk of catastrophic disaster."[13] Here Žižek appreciates the Maoist Badiou who argues, "better a disaster of fidelity to the Event than a non-being of indifference towards the event."[14] So following Beckett Žižek believes, "after one fails, one can go on and fail better."

Given what we have witnessed I cannot accept such formulations. They are ethically bankrupt and yet this is how Žižek would like us to proceed. He writes, "I know very well that things are horrible in the Soviet Union, but I nonetheless believe in Soviet socialism."[15] Such a thought according to Žižek is "the innermost constituent part of every ethical stance."[16] If it is part of every ethical stance to believe in such a disavowal then such an ethics needs to be abandoned for the sake of justice.

The simple question to ask Žižek is, "what have you disavowed?" Since I witnessed first-hand the brutality of war while I was in Croatia and Bosnia-Hercegovina I cannot go on "living as usual." Žižek loves to take examples from film and fiction. He writes, "The neighbour is the (evil) Thing which potentially lurks beneath every homely human face, like the hero of Stephen King's *The Shining*, a gentle failed writer, who gradually turns into a killing beast, and, with an evil grin goes on to slaughter his entire family."[17]

Think here of Stalin and Mao who killed with such polite civility. Žižek wants to assert that "there is an inhuman core in all of us."[18] He sees the person as a mask that conceals the "the pure subjectivity of the neighbour."[19] If we are to be saved it is not from those who pose as humans. Žižek cites a scene from *Break-Up* where Jennifer Anniston replies to Vince Vaughn: "I don't want you to wash the dishes—I want you to *want* to wash the dishes." The reason totalitarian marriages and regimes function

12. Ibid., 13.

13. Ibid.

14. Ibid.

15. Ibid., 14.

16. Ibid.

17. Ibid., 16.

18. Ibid., 17.

19. Ibid., 16.

is because there are those who *want to want to do*. Žižek sees Anniston's demand as "terrorist" which it is of course, because it "regulates" not only what you do, but also your desires.

Žižek is against torture but for different reasons. He writes, "this is why the greatest victims of publicly admitted torture are all of us, the public that is informed about it. We should all be aware that some precious part of our collective identity has been irretrievably lost."[20] Žižek continues with his Hegelian inversion: the victims of torture are not those actually being tortured, the victims are the public who now know what has taken place. Žižek mourns the trauma inflicted on "our precious collective identity." Since there is no such thing as a collective identity, it makes no sense to insist that it has been traumatized.

Stalin and Mao want to claim that no individuals were harmed in the glorious revolution and in the great leap forward since individuals do not exist for them. Only the class was targeted. The repetition that Žižek urges is not Kierkegaardian as he claims. It is, to cite Hegel, "the repetition of a conjuring trick already seen through,"[21] or as another line from Hegel makes clear, "When we wish to see an oak with its massive trunk and spreading branches and foliage, we are not content to be shown an acorn instead."[22] It is necessary to ask Žižek where the meat is as he proceeds to crack Lacanian nuts in an attempt to make the Master signifier rise.

Derrida's critique is clear. Lacanian psychoanalysis wishes to impose a master-signifier that is immune to the effects of dissemination. But such a signifier does not exist. In Nietzsche's language, the sun is also a star.

The imposition of a master-signifier hegemonizes symbolic space. We have seen how this imposition plays itself out. Žižek argues that Lacan's theory "can be used to throw new light on numerous politico-ideological phenomena bringing to the fore the hidden libidinal economy that sustains them."[23] Speaking of the Maoist Cultural Revolution, Žižek writes, "what matters was not the brutal violence and terror in China but the enthusiasm fired up by this spectacle amongst Western observers."[24]

Notice how the philosophers have failed us. Kant was enthusiastic about the French Revolution. Heidegger was enthusiastic about National

20. Ibid., 55.

21. Hegel, *Phenomenology of Spirit*, 52.

22. Ibid., 12.

23. Žižek, *In Defence of Lost Causes*, 100.

24. Ibid., 108.

Socialism. Foucault was enthusiastic about the Iranian revolution. Žižek is enthusiastic about the Soviet revolution. There is so much enthusiasm to trickle down the centuries as long as somebody else's head is on the chopping block. Žižek wants to capture the pure potential of revolt and to harness its enthusiasm in the service of radical transformation.

The obvious problem is not Žižek's good-natured heart that throbs for the welfare of humanity but the fact that no enthusiasm can emerge from a project that contains such a vicious beginning. Quite simply Žižek needs to look into the dead eyes of all the corpses lying at the feet of his masters like I did in Vukovar and then perhaps he would stop with his absurd theorizing.

If Žižek is equipped with full knowledge, unlike Heidegger and Foucault who "did the right thing for the wrong reasons" why does Žižek fail to act on the basis of his knowledge? Is the answer not given by Žižek's description of how liberal critics ridiculed Foucault? It would be, "yet another chapter in the sad saga of Western radical intellectuals projecting their fantasies onto an exotic zone of turbulence."[25]

In his chapter "On Revolutionary Terror from Robespierre to Mao," Žižek follows Alain Badiou's defense of "the politics of revolutionary justice."[26] Žižek argues, "Radicals are [. . .] possessed by what Alain Badiou calls the 'passion of the Real': if you say A—equality, human rights, and freedom—you should not shirk from its consequences and gather the courage to say B—the terror needed to really defend and assert the A."[27]

The only question to ask is was Žižek on the front lines defending equality, human rights and freedom when the Yugoslav Army was inflicting its brand of terror on the citizens of Slovenia? Did he fail to act because he actually wanted the Yugoslav Army to "liberate" Slovenia from its capitalistic aspirations? Žižek sees Robespierre "as a true peace-lover who ruthlessly denounces the patriotic call to war."[28] I fail to see how Robespierre institution of terror as a legal policy makes him a "true peace-lover." "Terror is nothing more than speedy, severe and inflexible justice; it is thus an emanation of virtue; it is less a principle in itself, than

25. Ibid., 115.
26. Ibid., 7.
27. Ibid., 158.
28. Ibid., 161.

a consequence of the general principle of democracy, applied to the most pressing needs of the *patrie*."[29]

Using the guillotine to create a "republic of virtue" shows the inhuman element of Robespierre's thought and practice. Žižek has nothing but praise for Robespierre who in the words of Lacan, confronts, "the latent monstrosity of being-human."[30] Robespierre claimed "I say that anyone who trembles at this moment is guilty, for innocence never fears public scrutiny"[31] is prophetic.

Robespierre trembled when his moment of public scrutiny arrived. But Žižek's Hegelian "switcheroo" tells us that Robespierre actually means to say, "the fear of being accused of treason is my treason because even if I 'did not do anything against the revolution' this fear itself, the fact that it emerged in me, demonstrates . . . that I experience the 'revolution' as an external force threatening me."[32] This is a cheap reading of the situation. In a revolution everyone should be fearful of the mob because it lacks the ability to think. Žižek always prefers to speak of the background from which we should understand a situation. We should forget the background and focus on the thing itself. The innocent had good reason to fear Robespierre as he set the blade of his Public Safety Committee slicing.

According to Žižek's reading, Mao for example, is not inhuman when he ruthlessly decided "to starve tens of millions to death in the late 1950s."[33] No, Žižek believes that Mao was delivering, "a simple and touching message of courage . . . the small will become big."[34] Žižek goes on "this terror is nothing less than the condition of freedom."[35] To back up this claim, Žižek cites the words of Yamamoto Jocho, a Zen Buddhist priest who writes that the warrior should, "consider himself as dead."[36] Here Žižek misreads Zen. The warrior monk is not a walking corpse who removes himself from the living. Žižek's reading allows him to plug the walking dead theme into his reading of Bryan Singer's film *The Usual Suspects* where Keiser Soeze shoots his wife and daughter dead so that he

---

29. Linton, "Robespierre and the Terror,"

30. Žižek, *In Defence of Lost Causes*, 166.

31. Ibid., 167.

32. Ibid., 167.

33. Ibid., 169.

34. Ibid., 168.

35. Ibid., 170.

36. Ibid., 168.

can, according to Žižek, "pursue the members of the rival gang mercilessly. [. . .] The Soeze-subject makes the crazy, impossible choice of, in a way striking at himself what is most precious to him."[37]

Striking at oneself is one of Žižek's favorite tropes of changing, "the coordinates of the situation in which the subject finds himself."[38] Little wonder that Žižek fails to practice the virtue of terror that he preaches. Žižek claims that instead of clashing with police, demonstrators at the G8 summit should attack themselves. I am waiting for Žižek to lead this group of self-flagellators and *Fight Club* groupies into action.

"Our task today," writes Žižek, "is precisely to reinvent emancipatory terror."[39] Terror never emancipates. One look at the pictures coming out of Abu Ghraib reveals the sheer idiocy of Žižek's position. This is why he can writes that Mao's murder of 38 million people is nothing more than "killing as part of a ruthless attempt to realize a goal, reducing people to disposable means—and what one should bear in mind is that the Nazi Holocaust was not the same."[40]

To be sure it was not the same. Notice how Žižek defends Mao. Mao's strategy according to Žižek was "rational" while Hitler's was "a meticulously planned irrational excess."[41] According to Žižek, Mao unlike Hitler was, "clearing a space and opening up the way for a new beginning."[42] Žižek prefers the Maoist solution because it was rationally ruthless. The only thing shown here is that many cannot think for themselves and, as Kant has shown, readily open their mouths waiting for the insertion of a new and improved controlling bit.

Merleau-Ponty's *Humanism and Terror* according to Žižek provides, "arguably the most intelligent legitimization of Stalinist terror . . . .as a kind of wager on the future."[43] As if to say that since the great Merleau-Ponty favored Stalin as did his compatriot Sartre, then it must be OK. Here we must be direct. Even if Jesus himself or God almighty agreed with Stalin and his policies we must reject such legalization for the sake of justice. Žižek writes that the wager is "almost in the mode of Pascal who enjoins us

37. Ibid., 170.
38. Ibid.
39. Ibid., 174.
40. Ibid., 187.
41. Ibid.
42. Ibid., 194.
43. Ibid., 224.

to make a bet on God if the final result of today's horror will be the bright Communist future, then this outcome will retroactively redeem the terrible things a revolutionary has to do today."[44] There can be no redemption of the in-human. The crimes committed by the revolutionary have never resulted in a brighter future because the future does not exist. Crimes become holy acts only in the minds of psychopaths.

Here is Žižek's defence of Stalin. He writes, "a true Stalinist politician loves mankind, but nonetheless performs terrible purges and executions—his heart is breaking while he is doing it but he cannot help it, it is his duty toward the progress of humanity."[45] That such words can be written by a so-called philosopher is repulsive at best. No doubt the millions of victims created by Stalin should forgive him for his undying love toward humanity.

Stalin according to Žižek is a "genius."[46] In describing Stalin's "dekulakization" Žižek writes, "the goal was to liquidate them *as a class*, not as individuals. Even when the rural population was deliberately starved (millions of dead in Ukraine again) the goal was not to kill them all, but to break their break bone, to brutally crush their resistance, to show them who was the master."[47] Merely writing "*as a class*" in italics does not erase the fact that individuals were murdered. Class is an invention used to hide the murder of individuals.

Imagine the Stalinist politician declaring, "We did not murder any individuals. Millions did not die. No individuals were harmed in the revolution since we decreed that they do not exist. Only the class was liquidated." One should be attentive here to the danger that Žižek presents. The very system that brought death to 100 million individuals is now supported by Žižek. What can be said in response to Žižek's love of Stalin? A new beginning cannot be built from a faulty foundation. Žižek's great risk is like a baby in jolly jumper in-front of Uncle Joe, thinking that it takes risks when in fact it is securely fastened. A return to communism is not an answer to our predicament.

Here Žižek finally reveals what his hamster is—"the fetish which enables (him) to (pretend) to accept reality the way it is."[48] What Žižek

44. Ibid.
45. Ibid., 227.
46. Ibid., 257.
47. Ibid., 262–63.
48. Ibid., 229.

proposes is neither realistic nor viable, though he continues to uphold its viral effects. We quote Žižek and send it back to him: " Ok, enough of this muddle—we are in a difficult struggle in which the fact of our free world is at stake, so please make clear where you really *stand*." [49] Where does Žižek stand? Here he approves of Badiou when he confirms, " Badiou's motto that the only way to be truly human is 'to exceed ordinary humanity, tending toward the dimension of the in-human."[50] Žižek and Badiou urge us towards an "egalitarian terror."[51] In short, Žižek is without rigor. His is not provocative. Praising Lenin, Stalin, and Mao is old news.

Joseph Vissarionovich Dzhugashvili (aka Stalin) was a murderer, a sociopath, and a sadist. How such a person managed to rule is another question. Žižek's return to the failure of communism shows the extent of his intellectual bankruptcy. It is one thing to feel sorry for Stalin for having been beaten by his alcoholic father and yet another to praise the love of humanity that Žižek claims Stalin had when he was carrying out his genocide. Stalin, the man of steel, enjoyed what he did.

Žižek attaches himself to the corpses of his masters while the best American academic journals continue to publish his work. When Žižek responds to clear criticisms of his work, he reacts as if someone has threatened the frame of his fantasy space. This is precisely what Žižek's scholarship amounts to. Sadly, it has not prevented an entire academic industry from perpetuating the fantasy. If anything, this work will stand as a testimony that a Derridean was not fooled by Žižek's Hegelian and Lacanian fantasies.

As David Bordwell writes, "It's tedious to be lectured on morality and ethics from someone who casually announces petty acts of deceit like sneaking out of office hours or fooling gullible academics who are eager to take a master's words as a revelation."[52] Bordwell clearly shows how Žižek is mere pastiche and how anyone can engage in free associative film interpretation. Lacan is no more of an ultimate background than Plato. Bordwell is correct: "the regulative idea of a research community is respect for argumentation and evidence."[53] Žižek provides neither as he is locked into the fetish of Hegel's feedback loop.

49. Ibid., 385.

50. Ibid., 443.

51. Ibid., 461.

52. Bordwell, "Slavoj Žižek: Say Anything."

53. Ibid.

8

For They Knew What They Did

Now, however, am I out of service, without master, and yet not free.

—Nietzsche, *Thus Spoke Zarathustra*, "Out of Service"

Žižek's *For They Know Not What They Do* was first delivered during the winter semester of 1989-90 as a set of lectures to Slovenian intellectuals who Žižek claims "were the moving force at the drive toward democracy."[1] Žižek laments the erasure of that "unique utopian moment" when "all options still seemed open."[2] Rather than lament, one wonders why Žižek and his audience did not take to the streets for some "real" revolutionary activity. Delivering lectures on Lacan while Slovenia was on the verge of war is hardly an exercise that captures that "unique utopian moment."

Žižek, as always, tells us that his analysis should be read against the background of Marx, Hegel, and Lacan. The problematic feature of these backgrounds are never analyzed by Žižek. He simply accepts them as a fundamental truth. I am reminded of a wall of graffiti at the skate-park my son attends. The background is whitewashed by the Public Works Department only to be decorated again by dueling artists. The point here is that many seem to need a background that never changes before they can venture out and theorize safely. So, Žižek is on a skateboard without wheels and somehow he has convinced his disciples that he actually can ride the

1. Žižek, *For They Know Not What They Do*, 3.
2. Ibid.

revolutionary half-pipe. His writing proceeds as if he is already skating when he is merely playing a video game.

Žižek has become fond of quoting the scandalous words from Luke's Gospel: "If anyone comes to me and does not hate his father and his mother, his wife and children, his brothers and sisters—yes, even his own life—he cannot be my disciples."[3]

Žižek argues (of course) that Jesus's words "take exactly the same direction as Che's famous quote, 'You may have to be tough, but do not lose your tenderness. You may have to cut the flowers but it will not stop the spring.'"[4] Perhaps Žižek has seen the revolutionary poster where Jesus is pictured with a rifle over his shoulder looking much like Che Guevera.

The revolutionary violence exhibited by Lenin is called a "work of love" by Žižek "in the strictest Kierkegaardian sense of the term."[5] Freedom Žižek tells us, writing from his apartment, "is not a blissfully neutral state of harmony and balance, but the very violent act which disturbs this balance."[6] It is precisely here that we can locate what is wrong with Žižek's approach.

As a Hegelian he believes he can give an educated comment on everything under the sun, even on things he has never studied in depth. If scholars assert that Zen is peaceful, then Žižek will claim that Zen is about violence. If Gandhi is seen as an exemplar of non-violence, Žižek will claim that he was the most violent human being. Stalin who has more blood on his hands than all the dictators of the 20th century combined is seen as being full of Kierkegaardian love. How such massive mis-readings have been accepted as a sign of intellectual superiority is truly baffling.

In his article on Tibet published in *Le Monde Diplomatique*, Žižek argues that we should not pass judgment on China before we know the facts about Tibet. Žižek believes that "Tibet was not suddenly occupied by China." China according to Žižek, "often acted as a protective overlord." Žižek argues, "Before 1950 Tibet was no Shangri-La but a country of harsh feudalism, poverty . . . corruption, civil wars." Žižek does not blame China but Tibet's ruling elite "who prohibited any development of industry." Žižek

---

3. Luke 14:26.

4. Žižek, *For They Know Not What They Do*, xivi. It seems that Žižek forgets what Lacan asserts. In *The Other Side of Psychoanalysis* Lacan gives his student audience the following advice: "I would tell you that always the revolutionary aspiration has only a single possible outcome—of ending up as the master's discourse. This is what experience has proved. What you aspire to as revolutionaries is a master. You will get one" (207).

5. Žižek, *The Parralax View*, 282.

6. Ibid.

claims that "the cultural revolution which ravaged the Tibetan monasteries in the 1960s"[7] were carried out by young Tibetan mobs. Since the Chinese invested heavily in Tibet they have increased the "standard of living" and should by all accounts be grateful for this expression of benevolent Maoist generosity. The reason why many are on the side of Tibet according to Žižek is "Tibetan Buddhism deftly spun by the Dalai Lama" who "is a major point of reference of the New Age hedonist."[8] This New Age Hedonism according to Žižek is becoming the "predominant form of ideology today."

Žižek claims that that the Tibetans never had it so good. They should not rebel but be grateful to the Chinese Communists for another great leap forward. By the same token Slovenians should have been grateful to the Serbian Communists for bringing social prosperity to Ljubljana and Maribor. How the exercise of righteous violence against one's oppressor undermines the validity of Tibetans to rule themselves makes no sense. China has taken what does not belong to it. This is perfectly acceptable to Žižek. He writes, "Today more than ever, in the midst of this scoundrel time we live in, the duty of the left is to keep alive the memory of all lost causes, of all shattered and perverted dreams and hopes attached to leftist projects."[9]

Žižek is fond of blaming capitalism for all the ills that plague our culture. When a person eats breakfast at Tim Horton's, goes to MacDonald's for lunch and has dinner at the A&W, capitalism is not to blame. The question to ask is why are so many willing to accommodate themselves without thinking about their actions? Žižek who sells books, gives public lectures for a fee, and accepts money from American universities, etc., while lecturing about the evils of "global capitalism," shows us the truth of the situation. He is the poster boy for the benefits of global capital. He is simply living the life that elite Yugoslav Communists were used to living. Communist leaders in Yugoslavia who preached "brotherhood and unity" to the working class lived in mansions. Žižek's "theorizing" is broken. It is not revolutionary. There is nothing revolutionary about Lacan who argues we are not complete, there are gaps and inconsistencies that constitute our lives.

Here is what he says about the revolutionary group *Shining Path* the Maoist guerrilla insurgent organization in Peru: "Behind Sendero Luminino's endeavour to erase an entire tradition and to begin from the zero point is an act of creative sublimation, there is the correct insight into the

7. Žižek, "Tibet."

8. Ibid.

9. Žižek, *In Defence of Lost Causes*, 271.

complementary relationship of modernity and tradition: any true return to tradition is today a priori impossible . . . "[10] Revolutionary terror in Žižek's words is "an act of creative sublimation." This is one of the better euphemisms I have come across. Žižek continues, "So precisely when we are dealing with the scene of a furious crowd, attacking and burning buildings and cars, lynching people etc., we should never forget the placards they are carrying and the words which sustain and justify their acts."[11] This is pure Lacan. We need not focus on the actual but on the Letter which arrives at its non-intended destination.

Lorenzo Chiesa in *Subjectivity and Otherness: A Philosophical Reading of Lacan*, argues, "Lacanian psychoanalysis does not promote any specific Master-Signifier, however it clearly meant to pave the way for a new Master Signifier which is compatible with its ethics."[12] Derrida's critique of Lacan is clear. Lacan wishes to impose a Master-Signifier that is immune to the effects of dissemination. The Master-Signifier is hegemonic. Chiesa urges us to "ethically assume the inconsistency of the symbolic order."[13] Chiesa argues that that the subject should "struggle politically to establish the hegemony of this new symbolic."[14] This is why Lacan is precisely totalitarian in his method. It goes without saying that there cannot be a radically new event under the circumstances described by Chiesa. If one name for fundamental fantasy is Marxism as Chiesa acknowledges, then we have already seen how this Master-Signifier has played itself out in the creation of gulags, prison camps, and other communist entertainment institutions.

In his *On Belief* Žižek argues for an "unconditional ethical engagement." The ethical engagement that Žižek calls for is not the one outlined by Arendt. It is the one that Lenin and Brecht embrace. The action that Žižek calls for is not the *via activa* that comes out of a thoughtful *via contempliva*. Action understood by Žižek seems to involve getting revenge. Here Žižek quotes Brecht's poem "The Interrogation of the Good" as he ends his book *Violence*. Brecht writes, "Hear us then: we know You are our enemy. This is why we shall Now put you in front of a wall. But in consideration of our merits and good qualities We shall put you in front of a good wall and shoot you With good bullets from a good gun and bury you With a good shovel

10. Žižek, *The Universal Exception*, 26.

11. Žižek, "Language, Violence and Non-Violence," 3.

12. Chiesa, *Subjectivity and Otherness*, 191.

13. Ibid.

14. Ibid.

in the good earth."[15] Is this Žižek's solution to the problems posed by liberal democracy? Should we follow Brecht who gives the following advice in his poem, "To the Students. . ." Brecht writes,

Unless you pledge your

Intellect to fighting

Against all enemies of all

Mankind

Never forget that men like you

Got hurt

That you might sit here,

Not the Other lot

And now don't shut your

Eyes, and don't desert

But learn to learn and try

To learn for what.[16]

Here Brecht's poetry tastes like sawdust. In his poem "To Posterity" Brecht laments living in the dark ages, "He who laughs has not yet heard the terrible tidings."[17] The terrible tidings what communism has engendered. For Brecht violence is unavoidable. He urges us:

Think

When you speak of our

Weaknesses

Also of the dark time

That brought them forth

Alas, we

Who wished to lay the

Foundation of kindness

Could not ourselves be kind.[18]

15. Brecht, "Interrogation of the Good," quoted in Žižek, *Violence*, 39.

16. Located at https://www.escritas.org/en/bertolt-brecht.

17. Ibid.

18. Ibid.

Brecht urges us "to think" and like Žižek it is clear that no real thinking takes place in their works. In his poem, "Reply to Comrade Kuo-Mo-Jo," Chairman Mao writes, "Seize the day, Seize the hour. Our force is irresistible. Away with all pests."[19] It is interesting how failed poets manage to become revolutionaries who can hold millions under their thrall. As Lee Edwards writes,

> According to the authoritative 'Black Book of Communism,' an estimated 65 million Chinese died as a result of Mao's repeated, merciless attempts to create a new 'socialist' China. Anyone who got in his way was done away with—by execution, imprisonment, or forced famine. For Mao, the No. 1 enemy was the intellectual. The so-called Great Helmsman reveled in his blood-letting, boasting, 'What's so unusual about Emperor Shih Huang of the China Dynasty? He had buried alive 460 scholars only, but we have buried alive 46,000 scholars.' Mao was referring to a major 'accomplishment' of the Great Cultural Revolution, which from 1966-1976 transformed China into a great House of Fear.[20]

The French philosopher Etienne Balibar proposes the notion of *egaliberte* (the demand for equality and liberty that goes beyond any existing order). Isn't this notion best seen in the old slogan used by the United States Military: "Be all you can be!" So the Army promises you the freedom of the corpse and a college degree and all you have to do for a free education is kill for the military in States where weapons of mass destruction lurk. Žižek here is like *Dog the Bounty Hunter* who brings fugitives back to his Stalinist Christ with pepper spray.

19. Located at https://www.marxists.org/reference/archive/mao/selected-works/poems/poems34.htm

20. Edwards, "The Legacy of Mao Zedong is Mass Murder."

9

Tickling the Subject:
The Body without Anus

There is thunder enough to make the very graves listen!

—Nietzsche, *Thus Spoke Zarathustra*, "The Convalescent"

THE BLURB ON THE cover of Žižek's *The Ticklish Subject* claims that the text is the "long awaited systematic exposition of the foundation of Žižek's theory." The publisher continues to heap praise on the text describing it as "first and foremost an engaged political intervention advancing the burning question of how to reformulate a leftist project in an era of global capitalism." If only this were the case. Instead of practical advice on how to "supplement liberal-democratic multi-culturalism" we get more Hegelian theory.

Terry Eagleton's review of Žižek's book in the *Times Education Supplement*, deserves a few remarks. Eagleton writes, "In a typical Žižekian inversion, then, the spectral Cartesian ego is reborn, but this time as its exact opposite, the id."[1] Inverting the Cartesian ego is as revolutionary as eating Twinkies while on Weight Watchers. If following Lacan, reality is simply "the set of fantasies with which we fill in this constitutive hole at the heart of being,"[2] then revolutionary change cannot emerge from such a hole. To emerge on the other side of the fantasy's pathological gaps is not political.

1. Eagleton, "Method in the madness."
2. Ibid.

Žižek's books can be read as holy texts that promise more than they deliver. So we must guard ourselves against Hegel's "night of the world" that destroys person and haecceity.

The unconscious does not depend on the Cartesian subject for its insistence and more than it depends on Lacan or Žižek. During an episode of *CSI New York*, Mac reveals that he threw out all of his wife's belongings after her death except for one item: a beach ball. He kept it because it still contains her breath. The detective deceives himself just like the Cartesian subject is deceived. The cogito receives its own message in its true inverted form, that is, the cogito is not the victim of madness but rather the victim of its own deception.

The problem is that Žižek's theorizing exists within his own Kinder Egg examples. This is Mike Featherstone's reading. He writes, "regardless of the number of dolls, or the presence of the miserable plastic toy inside the Kinder Egg, both objects prove to be in the final analysis, empty shells that point to nothing but their own obsolesce qua condition of possibility of the revolutionary event."[3] The chocolate may be enjoyable, but Featherstone's analysis is absurd. Kinder Egg theorists cannot lead anyone beyond, "the Hellish conditions of the present."[4]

Featherstone is exact in how he treats Žižek's work. He writes, "I seek to follow Žižek's own strategy of philosophical buggery to redeem the profane materialism."[5] This talk of taking a philosopher from behind to transform the "hellish" conditions of our world makes as little sense as Lacan's thesis that the only successful act is the one that fails. Communism has already be-shitted the world and I suppose it only makes sense for Marxist theorists teaching in English departments to continue with the process.

The type of "philosophical buggery" described by Deleuze, Žižek, and Featherstone does not result in any kind of conception—immaculate or otherwise. The only question to ask here is why is Žižek drawn to these fantasies unless to show us the "truth" of Sade who wrote, "the ultimate sexual pleasure is for a man to penetrate himself anally."[6] Žižek stages the Hegelian buggery of Deleuze, which he describes, as "the ghastly scene of the spectre of Hegel taking Deleuze from behind."[7] The obvious theoretical

3. Featherstone, "The Redemption of the Real," 309.

4. Ibid., 314.

5. Ibid., 295.

6. Žižek, *Organs without Bodies*, 48.

7. Ibid.

and practical question to ask is how would Hegel's ghost take Deleuze? Do these formulations really make Žižek into "a critic of great daring."

Žižek clearly misunderstands the Immaculate Conception. He asks, "how would the offspring of this immaculate conception look like?"[8] The Immaculate Conception refers to the Catholic notion that Mary, the Mother of Jesus was born without original sin. It does not refer to a "holy fuck." So, what does it mean to penetrate a concept? In Žižek's worldview it means to take everything and stuff it into a Hegelian-Lacanian machine. The outcome is nothing more than a pathetic Captain Ahab who risks the life of his entire crew so that he can ride Moby Dick. For some strange reason we see this pattern of giving up our power to others without much protest. We would rather, it seems, go all the way into failure rather than cut our losses and abandon what no longer works.

As Adam Kirsch aptly observes, "Under the cover of comedy and hyperbole, in between allusions to movies and video games, he is engaged in the rehabilitation of many of the most evil ideas of the last century. He is trying to undo the achievement of all the postwar thinkers who taught us to regard totalitarianism, revolutionary terror, utopian violence, and anti-Semitism as inadmissible in serious political discourse. Is Žižek's audience too busy laughing at him to hear him? I hope so, because the idea that they can hear him without recoiling from him is too dismal, and frightening, to contemplate."[9]

From the level of the Hegelian bone that Žižek favors, a very different picture emerges than the one he paints for his readers and groupies. Capitalism was already functioning within the communist system. It could be seen in the vibrant underground economy that allowed Yugoslav proletariats to survive. It was evident in the travels of the Gastarbeiters living in West Germany for extended periods of time, away from their families. German capitalism kept a large portion of Yugoslav citizens mindful of a better future. It is simply not true, that "the people longed for simplicity and sincerity"[10] as Žižek asserts. The promises of communism showed themselves to be lies. Communism failed according to Žižek because of its "primitive ideological indoctrination." It was already a failure from the very beginning of its birth.

8. Ibid.

9. Kirsch, "The Deadly Jester," 37.

10. Žižek, "20 Years of Collapse."

Along these lines the best criticism of Žižek's work can be found in an article written by David Pickus entitled, "Did Somebody Evade Totalitarianism? On the Intellectual Escapism of Slavoj Žižek."[11] Pickus shows how Žižek "does not deliver the insights that he repeatedly promises."[12] Pickus shows how Žižek's intellectual escapism is "is appealing (to those who like it) because it masquerades as boldness and depth."[13] Even Žižek's followers are caught in the game. On the back cover of *Did Somebody Say Totalitarianism* we read that Žižek explores, "totalitarianism in a Wittgensteinian way." Pickus writes, "it defies credibility to think that Wittgenstein would consider Žižek's prose an advance in lucidity and aptness or a liberation from the bewitchment of language."[14]

Pickus shows that "someone confident in his insights would not need to write so vaguely and obscurely or jump so erratically among topics. It is not a bold but a timid writer who takes refuge in such evasions."[15] In short, Žižek does not think carefully, reflectively, or seriously. What he offers is the same thing that Lacan offered his patients: overpriced mini-sessions that made the master rich but did not ease the suffering of those who sat at his feet.

Žižek's revolution is nothing more than a spin along the same old orbit. Žižek's supporters[16] will claim that "his message is at a higher level than any argument levelled against him."[17] The message of Žižek's work is that it has no message. It is a cannibalistic monologue. Laclau characterized debating with Žižek as a "dialogue of the deaf."[18] Laclau is clear, "If he does not want to be utterly misunderstood, he should be more careful in choosing his words when making a public statement."[19]

Žižek thinks that he is providing us with great insights on how the world works by looking at films. For example in commenting on Coppola's *Apocalypse Now*, he writes that the ultimate horizon of the film shows us

11. Pickus, "Did Somebody Evade Totalitarianism?," 146–67.

12. Ibid., 146.

13. Ibid.

14. Ibid., 154.

15. Ibid., 155.

16. Adrian Johnston, for instance, has written a number of books defending Žižek's work in a manner even more convoluted than Žižek's own ramblings. See esp. *Žižek's Ontology*.

17. Pickus, "Did Somebody Evade Totalitarianism?," 164.

18. Laclau, "Why Constructing a People is the Main Task of Politics," 646.

19. Ibid., 677.

"how Power generates its own excess. [. . .] Willard's mission to kill Kurtz is non-existent for the official record."[20] When my father's platoon went on patrol in the Adriatic they were officially non-existent. I fail to see how such a thing shows us that "power generates its own excess." Kurtz had no power. He was given power by those who welcomed him into their jungle lair. The fact that Willard kills Kurtz easily shows us that power is impotent. But watching *Finding Nemo* and applying a Lacanian interpretation of it will not result in the great Act or Event that will establish a better world.

If Lacanian theory can only celebrate a lack, then any politics derived from this theory is already a failure. In the end Žižek can only assert, "violence is needed."[21] Žižek reduces the human person to an excremental subject that remains constipated because it cannot break out "of the constraints imposed by an oppressive reality."[22] His Marxist moralization is given while he lives out the capitalist dream. This shows us that he mirrors the very thing he purports to denounce.

20. Žižek, *Violence*, 175.

21. Žižek, *Organs without Bodies*, 381.

22. Ibid.

10

A to Ž: (Discarded Ab-stracts From a Foreign Alphabet)

But I must ask you, Socrates, what do you suppose the upshot of all this? As I said a little while ago, it is the scrapings and shavings of argument, cut up into little bits.

—Plato, *Greater Hippias* 304a

I shall enlighten you, my amiable friends, as to why such disaster overtook you.

—V. I. Lenin, "Left Wing Childishness," May 5, 1918

GIVEN THAT ALAIN BADIOU has taken to acting in his own plays I thought I might contribute to the genre with my own screenplay. Here it is presented under the letters of the Croatian alphabet.

I do believe that using Lacanian theory to analyze culture is equivalent to using *Dora the Explorer* to explain Hegel's system. At best, it is an exercise in uselessness. I imagine an interesting thesis could be written and defended at the European Graduate School that could compare Freud's *Dora* with *Dora the Explorer,* showing how imperialistic hegemony is at the heart of the capitalistic psyche. Dora's adventure with the monkey in red boots goes through thesis, anti-thesis, synthesis to arrive at another repetitious *aufhebung*: Forest, Lake, and Really Big Hill. Dora sings a triumphant song at the completion of her triadic task: "We did it, we did it." Hegel would be so proud.

While Žižek believes in the tremendous emancipatory potential of Hegel's thought, I tend to side with Kierkegaard and think otherwise. Here is Kierkegaard's refutation of Hegel and Žižek from the *Postscript*: "One learns something from Christianity, misunderstands it, and in new misunderstanding uses it against Christianity . . . as if Christ had been a professor and as if the apostles had formed a little professional society of scholars."[1]

In Žižek's many repetitious and recycled texts, Hitchcock is the ultimate Lacanian or Lacan is the ultimate Hitchcockean. Žižek takes a director's vision of reality and then claims that this is the way reality functions. Just because Kieslowski's films portray a Gnostic universe does not mean that the universe is Gnostic or that Hitchcock posing as the Ur-philosopher has really plugged his camera into *L' origine du monde,* showing us the way things really are.

The success of Žižek's method is evident. He has become quite successful in using Lacan to analyze film, horror stories, science fiction, politics, and pop culture. Since no one has paid much attention to Žižek's market practices, I will attempt such an undertaking. My thesis is simply this: Žižek is a comedian pretending to be an impenetrable political theorist/revolutionary pretending to be a comedian, pretending to be Hegelian who has read Derrida and Kierkegaard very badly.

In a very confessional mode, Žižek reveals that he "was not allowed to work in (his) domain, philosophy, until 1990." Žižek tells us that he spent many years not working in philosophy while having to endure the directives of communist institutional research programs in order to survive.[2] Here Slavoj confesses that he had to cede his desire and betray Lacan's teachings.

When it came down to the choice between loving Lacan with jobless hunger or "marginal sociological research" he chose the side of the Yugoslav Big Other: Marshall Josip Broz Tito. Hegel's heroine Antigone would be very disappointed. Žižek's books have given many graduate students a rest from what passes as critical theory in North America. No doubt, he is fun to read. He is extremely entertaining as a lecturer.

Here is what I imagine as I think of Hitchcock while reading Lacan with my left eye and Žižek with my right.

1. Kierkegaard, *Concluding Unscientific Postscript,* 215.
2. See Žižek, "Critical Response."

A to Ž: (Discarded Ab-stracts From a Foreign Alphabet)

Here are the breakdown of scenes. Read them as discarded abstracts from a foreign alphabet:

A

Decades of engaging in meaningless Yugoslav sociological research and looking at huge portraits of Marshall Tito teach him the art of patience as he listens to Beethoven, Mozart, and Lai-Bach, watches Hollywood films and crafts books with witty titles. He battles with the ghosts of his parents—both committed to the cause. He hears the voices of his professors urging him to read more Marx and actually cite him in his thesis while he prefers to watch more Hollywood movies. Somehow he manages with the imposed universalism of one type of laundry soap, one flavor of ice cream, and one kind of coffee. Shall he star in a new *Groundhog Day* to become a repetition of the weatherman who must decide whether his life needs a Pauline renewal?

B

He buries his manuscripts in the floorboards of his State funded apartment until the days that Slovenia will emerge from ex-Yugoslavia (where did it go?) to finally become free of Tito's self-management terror. The joke was "They pretend to pay us, and we pretend to work." Should we read Žižek the way Stephen King describes his work? King writes, "My works are the literary equivalent to a Big Mac and French Fries."[3] It's only a burger. But billions and billions of assistant English professors in the United States are served.

C

Slavoj whose name means "glory" finally explodes on the scene of the capitalist West to save us from Chomsky, Strawson, Rawls, and Habermas as he emerges as "a startling critic of great daring." We ask, where was his daring and courage while Slovenia was still in the Yugo-Serbian dominated Federation? While he was a member of the Yugoslav Communist Party, Žižek did not stand up for his Lacanian principles. This would have meant a one way trip to Goli Otok (the Naked Island) where Tito imprisoned the politically correct. Imagine Lenin teaming up with the Dog the Bounty

---

3. As quoted in Temple, "The Literary Equivalent of a Big Mac."

Hunter to capture elusive capitalists hard at work playing golf while their stock options diversify.

Č

My Lacanian question to Žižek in clear Croatian is, "Zakaj ste (why did you), Slavoj cede your desire?" He might answer, "I was not ceding my desire. I was seeding my desire by writing speeches for the Party, reviewing films that I had never seen, writing reviews for books that were never published." In the Communist era the government paid the salaries of theater companies and athletes. Box office prices were low. Everyone could afford to go to the theater, movies, the opera, the ballet, or sporting events. What a blessing! Comrades were allowed to make their own whisky. The reasoning was simple: A drunken populace numbed on slivovitz cannot revolt. Stripped of his Kierkegaardian wit, jokes, references to Hegel, pop culture, and interesting book titles, what is Žižek actually saying? Can he be pinned down? Can his writings, following Baudrillard's fine phrase, be read as a "trans-aesthetics of banality?" Think here of the Prada Spring 1999 collection: handbags adorned by the faces of Mao and Lenin.

Ć

Shall we meet him next to the Louvre pyramid together with Tom Hanks to pay tribute to Christian materialism, Courbet and Magdalene's "holy grail?" to ponder how God's babies kick the wombs of mortal women? Indeed, one wonders what Lacan was actually saying as we attempt to read him through Jacques-Alain Miller's reconstructions. Here is Hegel from the *Phenomenology of Spirit* speaking dialectically about Žižekian theory:

> The knack for this kind of wisdom is quickly learned as it is easy to practice; once familiar, the repetition of it becomes as insufferable as the repetition of a conjuring trick already seen through . . . . . .
> It would be hard to decide which is greater in all this, the causal ease with which everything in heaven and on earth is coated with this broth of color, or the conceit regarding the excellence of this universal recipe: each supports the other. What results from this method of labeling all that is in heaven and earth with the few determinations of the general schema, and pigeon-holing everything in this way, is nothing less than a "report clear as noonday" on the universe as an organism, viz., a synoptic table like a skeleton

with scraps of paper stuck all over it, or like the rows of closed and labeled boxes in a grocer's stall.[4]

In other words, Lacan explains everything. Everything in heaven and on earth is coated in the same broth of color. Let us therefore eat from the excellence of this universal recipe. Look Hamlet, here is the skeleton of the decentered Self.

D

What is worthy of being an object of thought as we pursue the Lacan's Real? Whereas Hegel argues, "The True is the Whole," Lacan argues the Real reveals the hole. The Real is the grimace of reality. For example, an index finger with excrement on it. A dead raccoon on the smooth asphalt. The black spot on Jack Sparrow's palm in *Pirates of the Caribbean*, opening into a mouth, is a sign of traumatic excess. The noumenal shines through into the phenomena like bananas on the black market in Communist Yugoslavia.

Đ

I wonder why Žižek calls for a REPEAT of Lenin which according to him does NOT mean a RETURN to Lenin. Žižek claims that to repeat Lenin is to accept that "Lenin is dead," that his particular solution failed, even failed monstrously, but that there was a utopian spark in it worth saving. How do we pass judgement on the executioner who performs his duties with angelic conviction? Let us listen to Hegel describing Lenin and Stalin:

> The heart-throb for the welfare of humanity therefore passes into the ravings of an insane self-conceit . . . It therefore speaks of the universal order as a perversion of the law of the heart and its happiness, a perversion invented by fanatical priests, gluttonous despots and their minions, who compensate themselves for their own degradation by degrading and oppressing others, a perversion which has led to the nameless misery of deluded humanity. In this its derangement, consciousness declares individuality to be the source of this derangement and perversion.[5]

Here, Hegel makes so much good sense.

---

4. As quoted in Adorno, *An Introduction to Dialectics*, 47.
5. Hegel, Phenomenology of Mind, sec. 377.

E

I cannot take Žižek seriously especially when he writes, "To repeat Lenin is to repeat not what Lenin DID, but what he FAILED TO DO, his MISSED opportunities."[6] Let us allow Lenin to speak, "But we say in reply: 'Permit us to put you before a firing squad for saying that. Either you refrain from expressing your views, or, if you insist on expressing your political views publicly in the present circumstances, when our position is far more difficult than it was when the white guards were directly attacking us, then you will have only yourselves to blame if we treat you as the worst and most pernicious white guard elements.'"[7]

Here we can imagine Lenin as the Energizer Bunny that "keeps going and going," leading us to the jaws of the wolf.

F

What did Lenin exactly fail to do? Should he have continued with his terror within the Lacanian refrain in his ear: "Do not cede your desire?" Did he fail to make proper use of his average intelligence? Should we follow his tireless energy, indomitable will and native political genius into the utopia that Žižek has prepared for us? Should we follow the Lenin that wrote horrible prose and willingly–even eagerly–turned to murder, terror, and brutal repression? Should Lenin, father of the Soviet terror be repeated and called *Abba*? Is Žižek advocating a kinder, gentler state sponsored terrorism: Lenin with an excessive generosity; Paul without the throwing of stones at Christians? Mad Max lives to ride again together with John Wayne down a burnt out Australian highway looking for the gasoline of the apocalypse while we wait for our bids to be accepted on eBay.

G

While Žižek wants to retain Lacan's theories without exception, he picks what suits him from other theorists without giving us a complete understanding of their works. For example, Lenin the father of Soviet terror is to be "resurrected" for his utopian ideals. St. Paul is to be retained for his "militancy" against the pagans, etc. An unbeliever who cannot give up

6. Žižek, "Repeating Lenin," found at https://www.marxists.org/reference/subject/philosophy/works/ot/zizek1.htm.

7. As quoted in Žižek, "What Is To Be Done (With Lenin)?"

Christian hope is a Heideggerian. Žižek's claims are preposterous, vacuous and foolish. This finally explains why many do are drawn to hear him speak: great comedians draw large crowds. But so do bullfights, soccer matches, and evangelical preachers.

H

On the one hand, I read Žižek for the entertainment value and nothing more. I know such an activity is not very productive. It is comparable to watching re-runs of *Star Trek* or *Maximum Exposure*. I know I should be reading more analytic philosophy. On the other hand, I find in his writing an obscurantism that needs the lucidity of a deconstructive catholic critique. In *The Fragile Absolute*, Žižek argues, "One of the most deplorable aspects of the postmodern era and its so-called 'thought' is the return of the religious in all its different guises: from Christian and other fundamentalisms, through the multitude of New Age spiritualisms, up to the emerging religious sensitivity within deconstruction itself . . . . the authentic Christian legacy is much too precious to be left to the fundamentalist freaks."[8]

Žižek is wrong to put Derrida's deconstruction in the same camp as "fundamentalism and New Age spiritualism." I agree that we must be on guard against fundamentalism as long as we have first taken the fundamentalist log out of our own eyes. Is there a laser surgery that could accomplish this? Put bluntly, Lacanian psychoanalysis cannot provide the foundation of a new political practice because it is ridiculously inadequate for the task of being responsible to persons in their unique singularity. Lacan's theories are therapeutically and politically ineffective.

Between 1917 and 1959 over 80 million people were murdered in the Soviet Union. For the Left these numbers are acceptable because following Badiou and Žižek, they were a necessary outcome of the "Truth-Event known as the October Revolution."

Žižek considers Lacan to be an enlightenment thinker but he fails to answer the question, what is the knowledge that can immunize us against ignorance? How does psychoanalysis excise the pathology within reason and the pathology within spirituality?

8. Žižek, *The Fragile Absolute*, 24.

I

On one level, Žižek is right to criticize New Age Spiritualism but he should include his own writings within that camp. It is one thing to watch TV evangelists for their entertainment value and yet another to actually believe them and "tuck in a love gift" as you wait to receive your miracle spring water that will cure your cancer along with your acne and fix your finances as you finally manage to find meet the Lord while travelling 240 km/h in the fast lane of the 401. You have seen the advertising signs: "CH CH. What is missing? UR. Come in we are prayer conditioned. This Son will not burn you." The interesting paradox is that cultural theorists actually believe "in" Žižek.

The rider that never appears in fine print of Žižek's book might read, "Of course Christianity and Marxism should go together, that is, if and only if Christianity is understood as a stripped down materialism." Who needs this? Secular versions of Christian ideas are like cyber-sex. There is no point. Watching Extreme Make-Over Home Edition illustrates the materialism at the heart of religion. A family becomes poor after the death of their preacher-father. The generous trades-persons trained in video appeal, arrive to erect a 5000 square foot luxury home. The family with tears of material bliss rolling down their cheeks cannot believe their good fortune. Their faith is assured. God does provide for his needy flock. Here is what Kierkegaard writes in his Journals:

> *Preaching of the Gospel*
>
> Parson: Thou shalt die unto the world. The fee is one guinea.
>
> Neophyte: Well, if I must die unto the world I quite understand that I shall have to fork out more than one guinea; but just a question: Who gets the guinea?
>
> Parson: Naturally I get it; it is my living, for I and my family have to live by preaching that one must die unto the world. It is really cheap, and soon we shall have to ask for considerably more. If you are reasonable you will easily understand that to preach one must die unto the world, if it is done seriously and with zeal, takes a lot out of a man. And so I really have to spend the summer in the country with my family to get some recreation.[9]

---

9. Kierkegaard, *The Soul of Kierkegaard*, 221.

Should we collectively cry out, "Roll back that bus?" When will the Void be revealed for what it is? Does Lacan or Schelling actually lift the veil so that the truth can finally be seen? Does R. D. Laing come closer to the truth when he asks, "How do you plug a void plugging a void? How to inject nothing into fuck all?" Is the Real really unformed ghastly matter so that there is something in God that is not-yet-God, not yet fully constituted reality? Such speculation can lead into a discussion of *Mad Max*. God does not send his avenging angels to destroy the evil people who happen to enjoy fast cars, free apocalyptic gasoline, leather and a little pillaging. God does not send his angels to help the people dressed in white, guarding their oil, decked out in hockey gear armor. God sends Mad Max his other son. Perhaps Nietzsche announces it best when he writes, "there is much filth in the world; so much is true. But the world itself is not yet a filthy monster."[10] Didn't Max come to realize this point? He wanted some gasoline and in the process gets turned inside out. His trials do not make him angry. He can smile even as he realizes the absurdity of his situation. He drives a truck whose great tanker is filled with sand. He thinks it is filled with gasoline. The veil is lifted. The truth is known. It's only sand that pours out; the sand of time keeps flowing. The sun keeps shining perhaps telling us that it is never too late to learn to live and how to be human. But Max does not get on the bus where the gasoline is stored safely away. He knows to beware of the Magic Bus and its Leninist driver who tells his passengers that he has a map to the Promised Land and that he knows the way there because he has a stack of post-card images and Bolshevik trading-cards.

Žižek's reading of Christianity is no better than the TV evangelists who chastise his virtual congregation for writing checks that their souls can't cash. Or in the words of one evangelist, "Jesus does not like bounced checks." This sounds precisely like Lacan who with his suspect reading of Freud and others in his seminars coupled with a two minute psychoanalytic session that allowed him to see at least eighty patients a day, became very wealthy. Apparently, Lacan did not cede his desire. Perhaps what is needed is a thorough understanding of rhodopsin, the compound in the pigment of our eyes that enables us to see. If only philosophy could corner the market on this *pharmakon*.

---

10. Nietzsche, *Thus Spoke Zarathustra*, 222.

J

What Žižek's fails to observe and this is symptomatic of his prodigious mis-readings (of Christianity and Derrida) is that the message of Christ is not the message of Coke Zero. Think of Jesus on the cross being offered Vinegar-Zero. (Drink it and your crucifixion pain will be numbed.) Of course, Jesus refuses. Alain-Miller is right to claim that Coke claims it is IT though it never actually is it. Christ claims he is IT. He claims to be the Real Thing. Believe at your own risk. Žižek is correct to claim that with Coke the more you drink, the thirstier you get. Christ says the opposite. "Jesus replied, 'I am the bread of life. No one who comes to me will ever be hungry again. Those who believe in me will never thirst'" (John 6:35). Žižek gets Christ wrong because he relies on Lacan for his theological insights. The Chinese Government is harvesting organs from Falun Gong prisoners. There is torture at Gitmo. Jack Bauer endorses the "truth-serum" of a Glock on 24. Morality is an after-thought. The rest of the time there is state-sponsored murder in the name of progress. Tragedy does not begin with Homer. It begins with the bubbling up of the cosmic soup from which we arose.

Trapped in the desert of the real in the Capitalistic desert of consumer dissatisfaction is it possible to take solace in Psalm 63:1 which states, "God, you are my God, earnestly I seek you; my soul thirsts for you, my body longs for you, in a dry and weary land where there is no water?" Is the dry and weary land where there is no water but only Coke to be called *Amerika* or—the-former-Yugoslavia? In Yugoslavia, the so-called Marxist cadre could offer graduate courses in how to be good capitalists, while those not convinced of Tito's gentle hand, i.e., the workers and those forced to be *Gastarbeiters*, recited verses from Lamentations, "Because of thirst the infant's tongue sticks to the roof of its mouth; the children beg for bread, but no one gives it to them." Those upholding the virtues of socialism in Yugoslavia were living like rich industrialists. We conclude that socialist economics failed because of its inherent inadequacy to meet the needs of its citizens.

This is a good description of the Yugoslavia my parents and I were born into but it could just as easily describe the hardship experienced by the children of Marx. I mean not only Karl Marx's children who went hungry and died of disease while he failed to work and labor for them and lived from Engelian charity, but all the children of Marx from China, Africa, Latin-America, Cuba, and Europe who continue to suffer. This is an ethical argument and explains my dissatisfaction especially for the so-called

Marxist theorists in North America and Europe who drink Coke in the air-conditioned offices of their English departments, while collecting their tenured salaries, wearing Marxist T-Shirts made in third world sweatshops, while telling us how the petit bourgeois capitalistic system is an abomination because of its inherent oppressive nature. Who is being fooled here? Though I am in solidarity with a certain spirit of Marxism (e.g., its Tommy Douglas Canadian New Democratic version), applied "Marxism" in its various guises (Leninism, Stalinism, Titoism, Maoism) has been an experiment of disaster. Is this the fault of Marx or just a case of bad reading on the part of those who really had no business interpreting Marx such as the locksmith Tito and the failed priest Stalin?

What made so many follow the blunderings and violence of such individuals? While travelling through "Yugoslavia" in the late 1980s I was struck at how absurd everything was. Perhaps the only way not to go mad in such a mad environment was to embrace the absurdity of situation by making sure to have enough packs of capitalistic Marlboro Reds and Kents to buy freedom if needed. In such a world the only thing that made sense was Lacan.

K

Žižek continues, "The key to this disturbance, of course, is the surplus-enjoyment, the object petit a which exists (or, rather persists) in a kind of curved space—the nearer you get to it, the more it eludes your grasp."[11] The Yugoslav faithful would declare from a very young age, wearing red pioneer scarves, "Comrade Tito, We pledge our allegiance to you." Tito was the *object petit a* that held the faithful in his grasp even from the grave. After Tito's death the slogan recited by the Party was "After Tito, Tito." This is the Yugoslav version of repetition. It is the repetition Žižek favors: "After Lenin, Lenin encore." A repeat of Lenin would be nothing more than a retread. Tires that are retreaded blow up quickly sending flying debris onto the windshields bank-owned vehicles. In World War I retread was Australian slang for a re-enlisted soldier. Aquinas writes, "Useless repetition is vain." Žižek should listen to Aquinas.

While Žižek bemoans art that exhibits, "frames without paintings, dead cows and their excrement,"[12] he fails to realize that this is precisely the

11. Žižek, The Fragile Absolute, 24.
12. Ibid., 25.

materialistic leftover and as art, is much better than portraits of Marshall Tito hanging in the bedrooms of the communist cadres who cry out in search of the object petit a: Da, druže, da! (Yes, Comrade, Yes!).

The sublime evidence of "Leninism" lies in the materiality of its corpses. Žižek writes, "The sublime Grail will reveal itself to be nothing but a piece of shit."[13] As a "fighting materialist" what else does Žižek have to offer us? Christ without the resurrection is just another rotting corpse that does not smell any better, even when sprayed with a Unamunian perfume.

L

Žižek seems to think we can have Lenin without Lenin, Stalin without Stalin, Uncle Joe without the sixty million corpses, full of Marxist wisdom, warmth and generosity. No one writes a manifesto to declare: "Cultural Theorists of the world . . . you can been duped. You have nothing to lose but bad theory." Many seem to have swallowed Žižek's theories whole, not realizing what they are eating—the thick gooey, slightly brown paste served in the film *Brazil*.

Žižek wants a repeat (encore) of what Lenin failed to do. Of course, cultural theorists in the United States are excited. They can have yet another tool from which to carry out an analysis of things that really do not matter such as reading "Lenin's Utopia through Badiou's footnotes in *Being and Event*" and "Little Red Riding Hood as an example of the struggle to overcome class distinctions." Conferences will be organized. Lenin's corpus will now be re-examined. His brain studied again to locate the site of his "genius." The Western Canon will now be interpreted anew through the repetition of what Lenin failed to do. New courses with titles such as "From Lenin's cap to Khrushchev's shoe to Van Gogh's Pipe to Castro's cigar" will be taught. Dissertations with such noble titles as "Lenin's Pauline Theology," as an overcoming of the pagan drives inherent in spirit's implication in the political opposition of Weltgeist and Weltanschauung with reference to Marx's "all that is solid melts into air" and Hegel's "spirit is bone" will be written. I hope that I am not the only one who recognizes the utter uselessness of such intellectual auto-fellatio that continues to be published at an unprecedented pace. Bacteria swim towards sugar and away from acid. How can humans learn this wisdom?

13. Ibid., 26.

Lj

Let's be really serious as we turn the dialectical wheel. We speculate. Christ dies and does not resurrect but Paul takes his place. But no one really notices. So Christianity leads to materialism which is "the permanent production of piles of discarded waste."[14] The bodies continue to fill the earth. The Master is the only one who profits. The rest of us remain as victims of death. So Freud's formula, "Wo es war, soll ich werden" (Where it was, I shall come into being) is to be understand as "Where it was, I, Lacan shall be." However, the Master Lacan cannot lead us to liberation. Just as the fundamentalism of Paul, who desires to be the Master and asks us to obey his orders as we repress our inner urges, can only offer us dead letters.

Žižek does not seriously consider the real legacy of Christianity. He writes, "The authentic Christian legacy (Paul's fundamentalist militancy from the Corinthians) is much too precious to be left to the fundamentalist freaks."[15] Which fundamentalist freaks? He weaves through Marx, Lenin, Stalin, Toyota cars, cell-phones, Coke, Khrushchev, Courbet, NAFTA, NATO, and films—*My Best Friend's Wedding, Woman in the Window, Blue,* and *Vertigo*—only to conclude how fragile the Absolute is:

> What is the Absolute? Something that appears to us in fleeing experiences—say, through the gentle smile of a beautiful woman, or even through the warm caring smile of a person who may otherwise seem ugly and rude: in such miraculous but extremely fragile moments; another dimension transpires through our reality. As such, the Absolute is easily corroded; it slips all too easily through our fingers, and must be handled as carefully as a butterfly.[16]

A repeat of Lenin? I imagine Lenin training for the demise of capitalism dressed like Brad Pitt in *Fight Club*. Lenin-become-anarchist who tells us that the culture industry offers only the illusion of genuine transformation much like Bo-Tox and collagen used to lure a potential partner.

M

Žižek continues,

14. Ibid., 40.
15. Ibid., 2.
16. Žižek, The Fragile Absolute, 128.

> One of the rumors about Kim Yong II is that he actually died in a car crash a couple of years ago, and that in recent years a double has replaced him in his rare public appearances, so that the crowds can catch a glimpse of their object of worship—is this not the best possible confirmation of the fact that their 'real personality' of the Stalinist Leader is thoroughly irrelevant, a replaceable object, since it does not matter if it is the 'real' Leader or his double, who has no actual power?[17]

The obvious counter-argument here is: so what? Recall Seinfeld's comment that people who read tabloids deserve to be lied to. Shall we adopt the same attitude and argue that those who hero worship and have no skills of independent reasoning, who are easily fooled by the double-hero-Master-leader who is nothing more than a failed-priest-locksmith-turned-"revolutionary," with no formal education and yet can espouse the finer points of Hegelian dialectic, supported by the West to become their puppet in a strange cult of personality, deserve their leader?

One hundred million people were killed this century by communist regimes. This is solid evidence against its repetition. Yet, despite all the death and destruction left in its wake, communism still is viewed by Žižek and Badiou as a noble cause, the murder committed in its name simply an oversight. Thus Lenin and Mao (and presumably Stalin and Kim Jong Il) are good. Having witnessed evil several times in my life I recognize its face. I saw what Leninism, Titoism, Milosevicism, amounted to when I saw the mass graves at Vukovar. Simply put, it is a lie that Lenin dedicated his life to one thing and one thing only—the establishment of a society free from all forms of oppression. Lenin like other dictators from across the Left-Right spectrum filled graves.

Perhaps Žižek and Badiou and the rest of the Lacanians could visit Lenin's tomb and help the embalmers who periodically change his suit and bathe his body in a special chemical preparation to prevent tissue decay. Nikita Mikhalov, an eminent film director and chairman of Russian Cultural Foundation, says that vast funds are squandered away every year to maintain a "pagan show."[18]

---

17. Quoted from "Attempts to Escape the Logic of Capitalism: On the Political Tragedy of Vaclav Havel," by Slavoj Žižek, located at: http://www.lacan.com/zizek-capitalism.htm.

18. See Punj, "The Time Has Come to Bury Lenin."

N

Žižek's writings show us what happens when dialectical exuberance gets the better of kulak common sense. When I read Žižek, Lenin, Mao, or Lacan, I recall the question the Epicurean and Stoic philosophers posed to Paul: "What does this babbler want to say?" As Žižek addresses the audience of philosophers, bored liberals, theorists, film junkies, and disillusioned communists, I imagine him saying:

> My fellow Leninists and Lacanians I see how extremely perverse and obscure you are in every way. For as I went through the city and look at the objects of your desire, as I located your sinthome within the Borromean knot of the Imaginary, Symbolic, and Real, I found among them an altar with the inscription 'to an unknown god.' What therefore you worship as unknown thus I proclaim to you as the objet petit-à.

The applause of graduate students and those filling their CVs becomes deafening.

Let us locate the Paul that Žižek would find appealing, the Paul without Paul, the Saul of Paul, the Leninist revolutionary that mothered a religion, now into its third millennium. In Paul I find a universalism that fails to respect singularity. It is no wonder that theorists like Badiou return to Paul.

We can follow Žižek's Pauline materialism by substituting a few words in Paul's letters in order to create a Leninist speech that would make Stalin and Mao envious. Here is the result:

"Greet those workers in the revolution. I urge you comrades to keep an eye on those who cause dissension and offences. Now I appeal to you . . . that all of you be in agreement and that there are no divisions among you, but that you are united in the same mind and the same purpose. Not many of you were wise by human standards but the Party chooses what is foolish in the world to shame the wise. I feed you with milk from the farm, not solid food from the Big Box Stores, for you were not ready for solid food. I appeal to you then, be imitators of me. For the revolution depends not on talk but on power. Make no provisions for the flesh, to gratify its desires. Drive out the wicked petty bourgeois from among you. I wish that all were as I myself am. I have become all things to all people that I might by all means save some. Just as we have borne the image of the man of dust, we will also bear the image of the proletariat. Greet one another with a materialist kiss . . . . let anyone be accursed who has no love for the Party.

We are treated as impostors, and yet are true. Do not be mismatched with unbelievers. Indeed we live as human beings but we do not wage war according to human standards, for the weapons of our warfare are not merely human but they have materialistic power to destroy strongholds. I am talking like a madman. I have been a fool! You have forced me to it. Friends, I beg you become as I am, for I also have become as you are. My little comrades, for whom I am in the pain of childbirth until the Party is formed in you. Remember my chains. Anyone unwilling to work should not eat. For if someone does not know how to manage his own household how can he take care of the State? Teach and urge these duties; whoever teaches otherwise and does not agree with my sound words are conceited, understanding nothing, and has a morbid controversy and disputes about words. From these come envy, dissension, slander, base suspicion and wrangling, among those who are depraved in mind. No one serving the army gets entangled in everyday affairs. Avoid profane chatter for it will lead people into more and more impiety, and their talk will spread like gangrene. Obey your leaders and submit to them."

Paul like Lenin argues against dissension and individual expression. He wants imitation, not of Jesus, but of himself. Paul's gospel, which Nietzsche was correct to criticize in the *Anti-Christ* (because it forgot the message of the generous evangelic Jesus), may be summed up with the slogan, "No critique, or your eternal life."

0

The notion of *Denkverbot* runs through Paul's gospel and a repeat of Lenin as Žižek suggests is a return to not being allowed to think. Yes, Žižek is correct to argue that "today, actual freedom of thought must mean the freedom to question the predominant liberal-democratic post-ideological consensus—or it means nothing."[19] However, Žižek forgets that such a questioning is the foundation of a liberal-democracy. A repeat of Lenin is already a repeat of intolerance and repression. What Žižek sells to the liberal academy as radical chic, "Well, I have run out of ideas . . . . so let's repeat Lenin," is easily recognized by the most uneducated peasant as poisoned wine.

19. Quoted from *A Plea for Leninist Intolerance* by Slavoj Žižek, located at: http://www.lacan.com/zizek-plea.htm.

P

Žižek continues, "to put it in Kierkegaard's terms, THE Lenin which we want to retrieve is the Lenin-in-becoming."[20] Žižek wants to repeat, "the Leninist gesture of retrieving the revolutionary project in the conditions of imperialism and colonialism" so that "we obtain the right to think again."[21] Here I rub my eyes in disbelief. I wonder how such writing passes through the peer review process? Are editors blind to history? Perhaps they understood that Žižek's paper would be on Lennon. Lenin pronounced in "Serbo-Slovene" sounds like Lennon. Listen to the chorus of the Lennonist revolution: "Imagine there's no countries/It isn't hard to do/Nothing to kill or die for/And no religion too /Imagine no possessions/I wonder if you can/No need for greed or hunger A brotherhood of man I hope someday you'll join us/And the world will live as one." This universalism of all voices on one line singing as one voice on the line is incapable of thinking personhood.

R

While Žižek calls for a repeat of Lenin, notice how he downplays the crimes against individual persons committed by Stalin and Mao. Žižek writes, "In spite of all its horrors, the great Cultural Revolution in China undoubtedly did contain elements of such an enacted Utopia," and "The Stalinist . . . .terror was a gesture of panic, a defense reaction against the threat to this State stability."[22] We have heard this type of "Yes . . . But" logic in defense of Fascism and here Žižek repeats it for the monsters of the Left. Žižek wants to retain the Leninist "Utopian spark" but what he fails to realize is his quest for a universal truth is the spark that lit the fires of misery and oppression. Lenin is more relevant than ever in our "era of postmodern relativism" since "truth is by definition one-sided." Notice here that liberal democracy is so oppressive that one can write bad articles ("A Plea for Leninist Intolerance") that can still be published in excellent journals (*Critical Inquiry*). In Lenin's time, good articles (criticizing Lenin) did not have a chance to be published even in bad journals. The writer was murdered. No obituary was published. This is the Leninist universal that contains no variety within it. We have been

20. Žižek, "Repeating Lenin."
21. Žižek, *Revolution at the Gates*, 195.
22. Ibid.

prepared for this universal through pop culture propaganda where the characters speak the same language, with the same tone and inflection.

Only a repeat of Lenin can save us now? We would be like the silkworm once again laboring for the State while dying of our labor. Today, the silkworm moth, like many workers lives only in captivity. Silkworms have been domesticated so that they can no longer survive independently in nature, particularly since they have lost the ability to fly.

S

Žižek continues his Leninist observations in "Human Rights and its Discontents." The absurdity of his position escalates. The Lenin who liquidated those who disagreed with him is now the Lenin who would save us to think. Lenin is now to become an educator. In Russell's words, "Such education does not aim at producing any mental faculty except that of glib repetition . . . .From such an educational system nothing of intellectual value can result."[23] Glib repetition is the repetition that Žižek would have us return to which is evident from his misunderstanding of Kierkegaard's position.

Russell describes his meeting with Lenin in 1920:

> Lenin was cruel. Lenin had no respect for tradition. Lenin considered all means legitimate for securing the victory of his party . . . He thought the world was governed by dialectic, whose instrument he was. Lenin seemed to me at once a narrow-minded fanatic and a cheap cynic. He explained with glee how he had incited the poorer peasants against the richer ones, 'and they soon hanged them from the nearest tree—ha! ha! ha!' His guffaw at the thought of those massacred made my blood run cold.[24]

I prefer Russell because he speaks the truth here. A repeat of Lenin would be a repeat of broken promises, stolen liberties, and Stalinist idiocy. One more turn to the dialectical wheel of fortune as the revolution is revolved. Instead of Vanna White we have Žižek choosing letters on a loaded board that spins out the same message night after night: R E P E A T L E N I N. The contestants and viewers have no hope of thinking anything new or challenging the preachers of nonsense with their lame and impotent conclusions. Nietzsche showed us that Christianity was already emptied of the message that Jesus proclaimed so that the skeleton that Žižek would like

23. Russell, Unpopular Essays, 38.
24. Ibid., 166.

to construct would be fleshed out with Lenin's nicely refrigerated Moscow corpse that marches on Ukraine.

Š

Žižek's reading of Kierkegaard's notion of repetition cannot be bent dialectically in order to make Lenin into something new. The repetition that Žižek argues for is "a repetition of the wrong kind." Repetition as understood by Kierkegaard occurs in the realm of the religious. Repetition points towards Religiousness B. Kierkegaard's example is Job who "despite everything is in the right." This cannot be said of Lenin, no matter how the dialectic is used by Žižek. Lenin was in the wrong. Žižek's new Lenin is not Job who was blessed and receives everything back twofold. The new Lenin recollected and already repeated is to be found in North Korea testing missiles over Japan.

In his *Journals*, Kierkegaard argues, "And what is it we now call 'humanism' It is a vaporised Christianity, a culture-consciousness, the dregs of Christianity . . . . . One ought to say to the humanists: produce 'undiluted humanism.'"[25] Žižek and Badiou go to Christianity in order to dilute it of its power. They then proceed to inject it into an ideology that has been discredited. Such a coupling, like Frankenstein's monster, is perhaps entertaining but useless. For example, Žižek writes, "So although St. Paul's particular message is no longer operative for us, the very terms in which he formulates the operative mode of the Christian religion do possess a universal scope as relevant for every Truth-Event; every Truth-Event leads to a kind of 'Resurrection'—through fidelity to it and a labor of Love on its behalf, one enters into another dimension irreducible to a mere service des biens."[26]

T

The most profound expression of repetition according to Kierkegaard is "atonement" To atone is to reconcile; "to bring together again," "to make reparation." How would Lenin ever atone for the crimes he committed? How would he make amends? Or was that already done by Gorbachev with Perestroika? Žižek wants Lenin to be saved and redeemed. As such, there can be

25. Kierkegaard, The Sould of Kierkegaard, 209.
26. Žižek, *Ticklish Subject*, 143.

no reparation for Lenin's victims but only for Lenin himself. The tone of such atonement does not ring very well because it is fall back into un-freedom. Kierkegaard argues, "In the individual, then, repetition appears as a task for freedom in which the question becomes that of saving one's personality from being volatilized and, so to speak, in pawn to events."[27]

Unlike Kierkegaard's single individual, Žižek's Lacanian subject of the gaping Real is an expression of the tormented psyche that can find no rest. It seeks to fill the gap of its misunderstanding with obscene pathological fantasies. Singing soprano, in a hail of bullets, while following one's desire into the professional arms of one's sex-starved sex therapist; while a nip and tuck of the Borromean knot finally yield happiness for all the desperate housewives as they ride their youthful gardeners on waves of valium induced suburban bliss; while their emasculated husbands perform further Abelardian self-surgery is one lesson of pop culture.

This obscene underground domain cannot be transformed by a repeat of Lenin, especially when Lenin's so called utopia became a nightmare whose blueprint still stains the ground in current world events.

U

Žižek's theories are insufficient to formulate a clear project of global change because they do not take the person into account as Derrida does. Emancipatory politics has fateful limitations, not because of any hegemony in the present global petty bourgeois capitalistic system, but because it sets limitations on how the person is to be understood. A repetition of Lenin would mean the putting into action of a violent orbit; a loop of supreme crime that repeats (not in the Kierkegaardian sense) its failure to achieve a respect for individual persons. Let us allow Lenin to speak. Here he is from the ever inspiring work, "The Impending Catastrophe and How to Combat it." Lenin writes, "Unavoidable catastrophe is threatening Russia . . . .Yet nothing is being done. Six months of revolution have elapsed . . . Absolutely nothing of importance has actually been done to avert catastrophe, to avert famine. We are nearing ruin with increasing speed."[28]

Here is a kernel of truth that we can pop in our capitalist microwave. If only Lenin had stated, "Yes, we are responsible for causing this catastrophe and now we will help to avert famine," he would have been worth repeating.

27. Kierkegaard, *Fear and Trembling*, 213.

28. Quoted from https://www.marxists.org/archive/lenin/works/1917/ichtci/01.htm.

However, Lenin raises the stakes of the dialectic. He increases the catastrophe. He aids in prolonging the famine. He turns up the volume on ruin while turbo-charging the speed of terror. What the young Marx described as the horrible working conditions of England, equally apply to the Leninist state: "the fantastic rags of the . . . .poor, and the withered wrinkled flesh of the women consumed by work and poverty; children lying in filth; monstrous creatures produced by overwork in the monotonous mechanism of the factories? And the most delightful final details of practice: prostitution, murder and the gallows!"[29]

Point 11 of Marx's "Points on the Modern State and Civil Society" declares, "The philosophers have only interpreted the world in various ways, the point is to change it." Point 12 might read, "The philosophy that thinks it can change the world by ignoring the single individual needs to be changed before there can be any change."

Leninism, Stalinism and Maoism not only tolerated the plight of millions of human beings who were grossly deprived of bread and water, equality and freedom, they aided and created the disaster. When Žižek and Badiou urge a repeat of Lenin, their call is obscene and unwanted by those who know what suffering is. Their ideology was an enemy of democracy and an enemy of humanity. What could we expect especially from comrade Stalin who began his career as a bank robber and extended his talents to secure funds for Lenin?

Here is the wisdom that Alain Badiou in his love for Mao and Lenin would have us embrace. In his essay, "One Divides into Two," Badiou writes, "Our duty, supporting ourselves on Lenin's work, is to reactivate in politics, against the morose obsessions of our times, the very question of thought. To all those who claim to practice political philosophy, we ask: what is your critique of the existing system? What can you offer us that is new? Of what are you the creator?"[30]

Lenin who is critical of the social democrat Karl Kautsky for upholding the right to vote, accuses Kautsky of making "litter our of theory." However, it is the case that Badiou and Žižek are making theory out of litter. We can answer Badiou. "A repeat of Lenin is a morose obsession that can only result in catastrophe, collapse, sickness, squalor, abuse, hate, violence and murder. This ideology or ideas translated into values must be fought against, especially in remembrance of the 100 million victims who were

29. Marx, "Kritische Randglossen," 396.
30. Located at http://www.lacan.com/divide.htm.

murdered as a result of Leninist ideology." Badiou offers us nothing new. He is not a creator, though he would have us become children of Lenin, our mother. Here we could learn a new proletariat prayer:

> Hail Lenin:
>
> The proletariat academics are with thee
>
> blessed art thou among revolutionaries
>
> and blessed is the fruit of thy womb, terror.
>
> Holy comrade,
>
> mother of many Stalins
>
> Pray for us,
>
> Now and at the
>
> hour of our internment in your Gulag.

The requests for our politics are simple as I take my bearings from the prophet Isaiah: to eat, to be clothed, to have shelter, to be able to work, to be loved, to be cared for, to live in peace, and finally to find compassion that overcomes competition, money and power. This politic would finally liberate us from Fascism, Communism and Capitalist servility.

As Derrida has taught us the present form of democracy remain inadequate to the democratic demand that calls for a respect of singularity. The current threats to our liberty must be fought against by maintaining the liberty of the question. Such threats include the powers of the electronic network that files our identities into easily retrieved bits of data to be used by police networks, bank, health and insurance agencies. These virtual networks extend the powers of theft, falsification. The choice is no longer between the right kind of papers but what is contained on the magnetic strips that carry our information. That is why he calls for a democracy-to-come which will always remain aporetic in its structure and not capable of being contained within the system of calculable knowledge. Derrida writes,

> Yes, like searchlights without a coast, they sweep across the dark sky, shut down or disappear at regular intervals and harbour the invisible in their light. We no longer know against what dangers or abysses we are forewarned. We avoid one, only to be thrown into one of the others. We no longer even known whether these watchmen are guiding us towards another destination, nor even if a destination remains promised or determined. We wish only to

think that we are on the track of an impossible axiomatic which re-main to be thought. Now, if this axiomatic which withdraws, from instant to instant, from one ray of the searchlight to another, from one lighthouse to the next (for there are numerous lighthouses, and where there is no longer an home these are no longer homes, and this what is taking place: there are no longer homes here), this is because darkness is falling on the value of value, and hence on the very desire for an axiomatic, a consistent or presupposed system of values.[31]

The truly different may not arrive as the good, the beautiful and the just, but their exact opposite: the real good, the real beautiful and the real just. The repetition that Žižek urges is old territory. There is no hope of redemption in the structures created by Lenin and Stalin. Delivered from Fascism we cannot allow ourselves a return to Leninism in the name of a false democracy. We cannot be content with what today passes for de-mocracy. Let us prepare to leave Žižek's fantasy space while we return Lenin to the anorexia of Barbie's world. Here the mythic revolutionary and embalmed hero could join with the thin, long-legged, luxuriously blond bleached buxom plastic beauty to teach China how to really make great leaps forward.

V

To keep up with this screenplay argumentation, I turn to Kierkegaard's *Postscript* to show how Johannes Climacus answered Žižek and Lenin, Sta-lin, Tito and Mao in 1846.

"The observer, world historically catches a glimpse of the play of col-ors in the generations, just like a shoal of herring in the sea—the individual herring is not worth much . . . He hangs up curtains systematically and uses people and nations for that purpose—individual human beings are nothing to him."[32]

and

"Therefore the Hegelian cannot possibly understand himself with the aid of his philosophy; he can understand only what is past, is finished, but a person who is still living is not dead and gone. Presumably he consoles himself with the thought the if one can understand China and Persia and

31. Derrida, *Politics of Friendship*, 81.

32. Kierkegaard, *Concluding Unscientific PostScript*, 159.

six thousand years of world history, then never mind a single individual, even if it is oneself."[33]

Is it really still necessary to explain these quotes to the Hegelian-Maoist-Lacanian-Leninists? Should I request a suitable remuneration for my meritorious service of finding a suitable quotation to help liberate them from themselves? What is the going hourly rate? Would they be capable of paying? Lenin can only be seen as an example of inhumanity. To treat human beings as worms is to assert that all they need is the dirt of materialism. This is Leninism. His regime was a criminal enterprise. Maxim Gorky contends, "Lenin and Trotsky don't have any idea about freedom or human rights. They are already corrupted by dirty poison of the power; this is visible by their shameful disrespect of freedom of speech and all other civil liberties for which the democracy was fighting."[34] Lenin's 1919 letters to Gorky contain threats: "My advice to you: change your surroundings, your views, your actions, otherwise life may turn away from you."[35]

Karl Kautsky in "The Moscow Trial and the Bolsheviki," (1922) answered Lenin with great clarity. His criticisms are correct: "There is no difference between a tyrant who lives in a palace and a despot who misused the revolution of workers and peasants to ascend into the Kremlin . . . From the very beginning, they founded their power upon falsehood and violence directed against the proletariat, upon the principle that the end justifies the means. This principle always and inevitably leads to the degeneration of the party applying it, for it perverts the party and paralyzes those who do not oppose this perversion."[36]

Z

In *Pirates of the Caribbean: Dead Man's Chest*, Davy Jones is portrayed as a cross between a man and an octopus, with a wriggling beard of tentacles. He becomes the Octopus-Man who commands the Kraken and a crew of undead sailors. Davy Jones' Locker is the bottom of the sea. It is the resting-place of drowned seamen.

33. Ibid., 307.

34. Quoted from https://en.wikiquote.org/wiki/Talk:Maxim_Gorky.

35. Quoted from http://www.visegradliterature.net/works/cz-en/Gorkij,_Maxim/biography.

36. Located at https://www.marxists.org/archive/kautsky/1922/xx/twelve.htm.

Davy Jones is the sea Devil in search of souls. He pursues a life of violence but his heart is locked in a treasure chest that beats for the love he lost. If only Davy Jones had not lost his love. Love lost turns not into hate but a love of hatred. If only Lenin's brother was not murdered, would many have been spared the infliction of terror?

Elizabeth Swan must choose between three swords while Jack Sparrow, Will Turner, and the Lieutenant must choose between three caskets. Our Hegelian choice is between the Real Pirates of her majesty's *East India Trading Company*, Sparrow's Pirates, or Davy Jones' undead crew. How to answer the question, "Who is the fiend?" Is it Jones who presides over the evil spirits of the deep? Is it the King for whom one gathers all the gold? Or is it God? Theory can be found in the most unlikely of places. At the end of the movie, Jack Sparrow leaps into the toothed opening of the Kraken. Shall he resurrect for yet another movie?

I am in front of Wal-Mart. A man sits on the curb smoking a cigarette next to the Propane Cylinder Exchange Station. I wonder if he can read the "No Smoking" sign and if he can make sense of the slogan "Spark something fun?" As I wonder why I am thinking about these things so close to witnessing a potential explosion, I want to ask him if he has read Lenin or Žižek . . . Yes, I should have told him to stop smoking. One spark can spark something fun: soccer, death the revolution, and the resurrection? Who is the fiend? The Buddhist says "desire" and "ignorance." On Stalin's birthday, prisoners would send him congratulatory telegrams from the gulag. Flour bulked up with sawdust in Ceausescu's Romania was his Stalinist gift to his people. Who will be the Antigone that will finally bury the body of Lenin?

Ž

If I had the time and energy, I would have examined all of Lenin's letters to his mother. I would have wanted to find the kernel that led Lenin to create his sophisticated apparatus of rule by terror. In one of these letters Lenin writes, "Please send me some money, mine is nearly at an end." Here the father of the Soviet Union asks his mother for money. I would have read this request together with Baudelaire's "Counterfeit Money" to form a thesis about Counterfeit Regimes. Along the way I would have also examined Lenin's question, "How can you make a revolution without executions?" and his fine article, "Beat—But Not to Death!" Recall Hegel's words, "Here shoots a bloody head—there another white ghastly apparition . . . one catches sight of this night when one looks human beings in the eye into a night that becomes awful."[37] What better description of totalitarian states and of the traumatic encounters that humans engender as they turn spirit into bone?

Žižek writes, "For Lacan . . . a Truth-Event can operate only against the background of the traumatic encounter with the undead/monstrous Thing."[38] Is this not an excellent description of Lenin's refrigerated corpse? What is Žižek's Lacanian lesson? Do not cede your desire—You may. You are ordered to be free. Dare. Dare from the Old English word durran means "to brave danger." To dare is to be bold. It means to challenge and to defy, especially when stupidity masks itself, to perform a stunt of great theory.

If the world is Lacanian, then the history of our species shows the pathological everyday stains of living in what is named and remembered of the last century when we say Hiroshima, Nagasaki, Auschwitz, Gulag, democracy, fascism, communism. Philosophy without an aporetic ethics.

> I am polite towards them as towards every small vexation; to be prickly towards small things seems to me the wisdom of a hedgehog.

—Nietzsche, *Thus Spoke Zarathustra*

37. Hegel, "Jenaer Realphilosophie," 204.
38. Žižek, *The Ticklish Subject*, 162.

11

Franciscan Persons and
the Slum Colonies

They meet an invalid, or an old man, or a corpse—and immediately they say: "Life is refuted!" But they only are refuted, and their
eye, which sees only one aspect of existence.

—Nietzsche, *Thus Spoke Zarathustra*, "The Preachers of Death"

IN HIS "NATURE AND ITS Discontents," Žižek claims, "the global capitalist
system is the substantial 'base' that mediates and generates the excesses
(slums, ecological threats, etc.) that open up the site of resistance."[1] Is this
really the case? Do slums exist as a result of "the global capitalist system"
as something exclusive to capitalism? If we define slums as a place where
persons are reduced to bare life, following Agamben's term, deprived of
rights, of necessities, of food, medicine and education then it is clear that
the slums Žižek's speaks of were prevalent, not as an excess, but as a result
of life under Communism.

Žižek's embrace of Communism as a solution to the ravages of global
capitalism would only return us to the slum of universality. For Žižek, "the
underlying problem is here: how are we to think the singular universality of the emancipatory subject."[2] Yes. This is precisely the problem. But
Žižek misses the Derridean point. The question should be "how are we to

1. Žižek, "Nature and Its Discontents," 37.
2. Ibid.

think the singular haecceity of the person?" Žižek wants to find a "new proletarian position"[3] among the inhabitants of the "slums in the new megapolises,"[4] but such a finding dooms the person to yet another round of violence and terror.

From his mistaken starting point of still seeing Communism as the key, Žižek writes, "While one should resist the temptation to elevate and idealize the slum dwellers into a new revolutionary class, one should nonetheless, in Badiou's terms perceive the slums as one of the few authentic 'eventual sites' in today's society."[5] I fail to see how an ethics of the event will take place in the slums of Mexico, India, China, Indonesia, Los Angeles, and New York when the problem of the slum is a problem of the city and how its spaces are organized. Do Žižek and Badiou really think a slogan such as "Slum dwellers of the world unite . . . ." will change the greed filled psyches of capitalists, current day communists and other totalitarian rulers?

Žižek writes, "a slum dweller is a homo-sacer, the systematically generated, 'living dead' an animal of global capitalism. He is a kind of negative of the refugee: a refugee from his own community."[6] The slums exist because persons are not properly taken care of. The city did not live up to its promises. Here the best example is North Korea.

In recent days, the Great Leader keeps coming up in my news feed. Today, February 9, 2016, the Great Leader had another of his army generals executed. I have spent some time looking at photographs of Kim-Jong-Un surrounded by his generals. The fact that he is still alive is difficult to understand.

The great Communist Leader has a personal net worth of 5 Billion dollars, yet his people are starving. 12 million North Koreans live in extreme poverty while his wife eats caviar and walks around with Dior handbags. Perhaps I overlooked that commandment in Marx's collected works.

North Korea, like all dictatorships, has an elite ruling class that denies its citizens a minimum for human survival. Other forms of government also have elite ruling classes that make use of the veneer of democracy to maintain its privilege, but for the most part, citizens of these countries are not reduced to bare life. The Great Leader spent $600 million buying luxury goods for himself last year, while his citizens went hungry.

3. Ibid., 40.
4. Ibid.
5. Ibid., 40–41.
6. Ibid., 41.

Žižek asks, "What is to be Done?"[7] No, not what is to be done about Kim, what is to be done about capitalism? Žižek wants a "strict egalitarian justice" combined with "terror."[8] This amounts to the solution that "all people should pay the same price."[9] He asks, "doesn't the ecological challenge offer a unique chance to re-invent the "eternal idea" of egalitarian terror?"[10] I answer No. Cutting off the heads of those already oppressed would not solve the problem. Since only the very rich can afford ecologically friendly devices, the only people who would be subject to Žižek's egalitarian terror would be the very slum dwellers he proposes to organize as the new Communist vanguard.

While preaching about equality, Žižek is really preaching to uphold the rights of the elites. The King's head need not fall at all; only the idea of the King needs to fall along with the need for thinking that one person is a king or royal or a queen or a prince while another is a servant, a maid, a junior footman or a butler or some other ridiculous invented distinction.[11] The TV series *Downton Abbey* where the aristocracy gets fat through its tuxedo illusions of domination is a great illustration of how elites live. Doesn't the uprising begin when the servant, in response to her Master's bell says, "Screw you! Make your own tea! I am not your dog!"

I think that Jacques Rancière provides us with a better analysis of Žižek's embrace of Stalin. Rancière sees democracy as a disruption of the prevailing police order. Rancière's democracy is not that of the liberal-democratic state with its parties, elections and basic oligarchic institutions. Democracy is the constant vigilance against the oligarchy of the state where the elected few, govern and control the many. Democracy as envisioned by Rancière occurs when the needs and values of person's become primary. His notion of democracy goes beyond the state and its structures and beyond capitalism that has achieved hegemonic control over all aspects of our lives. Democracy is a disruption of the bureaucratic status-quo, as it seeks to disrupt rule.[12]

---

7. Žižek, "Nature and its Discontents," 69.

8. Ibid.

9. Ibid.

10. Ibid., 70.

11. Here it is necessary to re-read Hegel's Master-Slave dialectic.

12. Rancière, *Ten Theses on Politics*, 6.

As Rancière makes clear, democracy unsettles the prevailing order without becoming institutionalized.[13] Democracy needs to confront the current police state. He argues that while the police are grounded on the shore, politics is mobile on the sea.[14] The police states protects the capitalist axiomatic. The people must pay for the sins of bankers and CEO's. They continue to proceed with their activities unobstructed. They continue to make millions because they have set up the rules of the game, while the spectators continue to fund their endeavors. The message is "Work hard little children and you too may come out on top!"

Rancière defines police as, "an order of bodies that defines the allocation of ways of doing, ways of being and ways of saying and that sees that those bodies are assigned by name to a particular place and task."[15] The point is that no one is excluded from order, place, role or position. Democracy is "the mode of acting that perturbs this arrangement."[16]

Žižek would have us turn to those who live in slums as a model. Take the 2011 riots that spread through London and other English cities. Zygmunt Baumann called the uprisings, "riots of defective and disqualified consumers."[17] Baumann was right. The protestors weren't asking for freedom, health-care or education. They wanted more stuff.

The inequalities between the rich and the poor increase with delay. The problem is not capitalism and the solution is not communism. The answer is the Franciscan notion of haecceity that sees individuals as persons rather than mouths that consume, anuses that excrete and thumbs that tweet their dissatisfaction.

Why do so many humans worship those who are in-human? Do the slaves in North-Korea actually think that Kim is a God? How could one possibly believe that Mao, Hitler, Stalin and Pol Pot would provide them with a future? If thinkers like Heidegger and Badiou were drawn in by Hitler and Mao's rhetoric, can we expect everyday people to resist the lure of totalitarianism? We in North American are not immune to folly either. The founder of Apple was allegedly rotten to the core but his devices keep on selling. Jobs was worshipped by millions, who thumbed their way

---

13. Rancière, *Disagreement, Politics and Philosophy*, 34.

14. Rancière, *On The Shores of Politics.*

15. Rancière, *Disagreement, Politics and Philosophy*, 29.

16. Rancière, *The Philosopher and His Poor*, 226.

17. Baumann, "On Consumers Coming Home to Roost,"

through their day looking down on their devices instead of looking at the world around them.

The real question of democracy is psychological in nature: How do we get rid of the monkey within us that is willing to sell itself out for a banana and some stock options? All the other questions are roads that lead to nowhere. We will not be able to find solutions like Žižek thinks we can by looking at Hitchcock films or reading Lacan through a Hegelian lens. His activity has inspired other scholars to seek fictive solutions to real world problems.

I take Olivia Burgess's "Revolutionary Bodies in Chuck Palahniuk's *Fight Club*" to be a great example of using literature to find revolutionary solutions to our current predicament. She writes as if Fight Club were actually real: "*Fight Club* uses playful subversion and rule-breaking to undercut and redefine the discourse of dominant society and contribute to an ongoing exploration of the social world."[18] Really? Burgess highlights all the key *pomo*-words that really say nothing useful, but the novel *Fight Club* does no such thing. Palahniuk's works have benefited Palahniuk's bank account. The novel no more contributes to the transformation of the social world than Žižek performing Sunday Mass in Ljubljana's cathedral.

When Derrida refers to an event worthy of the name, that is, something we cannot predict, something that takes us by surprise, something which is a unique singular occurrence, he is describing Persons. An individual follows the rule but a Person is the exception to the rule. What we are cannot be predicted, circumscribed, set in stone. What we are cannot be appropriated. It is unforeseeable. It cannot be, anticipated. It is a pure singularity that is exceptional, irreplaceable and incalculable.[19] Were Hitler, Stalin, Mao, Lenin, and Pol-Pot persons? Clearly not. They were in-human individuals who reduced life to a Procrustean model. In Derrida's words, they sought to have a single voice on the line; their own. The Person is a heterogeneity based on haecceity and not a heterogeneity that derives from a homogenous source. Here we are against John Millbank's work that desires a "pure and absolute social consensus."

Millbank's so called radical theology does not take us beyond the managerial society we are in—the administrative society of non-thinking drones where the political is reduced to policing and surveillance. This universal monism is already a fundamentalism. My postmodern ethics

18. Burgess, "Revolutionary Bodies in Chuck Palahniuk's *Fight Club*," 268.

19. Derrida, *Rogues*, 135.

declare that the state is not sovereign. The Lord, King, and Queen are not sovereign. The Pope is not sovereign. They cannot decide the exception. Here I am against Carl Schmidt's thesis.[20] I never agreed to be led by Shep and become part of his herd. Did you?

The Person is sovereign. The Person is s/he who decides the exception. Here Justice is allowed to speak the Truth to the *jouissance* of the Other, which is evidently absurd and non-factual. The right to irrationality stops when truthful evidence shows the bankruptcy of your position.

Žižek's answer to fight the system is given in his analysis of *Fight Club*. When Ed Norton's character beats himself up in front of his boss, Žižek says, "the fact of beating up oneself renders clear the simple fact that the master is superfluous."[21] For Žižek, beating oneself up is "the first act of liberation."[22] It is of course funny to realize that Ed Norton's character never beat himself up at all. It was all an act. No real blood was shed. Žižek would have us believe, "the same strategy is used in political demonstrations . . . the way to bring about a shocking reversal of the situation is for the individuals in the crowd to starting beating each other."[23] This is idiotic. Of course, since the proof is always in the pudding, I don't recall Žižek beating himself up when the Yugo-Serbian Army attacked Slovenia. He was, of course, hidden from real danger watching films and pretending that he had an answer to the stain of the Real flooding the streets of Ljubljana.

For Žižek, "masochism is the necessary first step towards liberation."[24] He continues, "our liberation has to be staged in some kind of bodily performance . . . .it has to stage the painful process of hitting back at oneself."[25] Since Ed Norton's character in *Fight Club* beat himself up to great effect *mutatis mutandis* it must work in real life.

In his recent book *Event: Philosophy in Transit*, Žižek comes close to the Franciscan position but then veers off into Hegelian abstraction. He dedicates his book to "Jela, the event of my life." Jela, Žižek's latest wife, is an event for him. Rather than describe why this is the case, Žižek gives examples of non-events in literature, film, and art.

20. See for example Schmidt, *Political Theology*.

21. Žižek, "The Violence of the Fantasy," 286.

22. Ibid.

23. Ibid.

24. Ibid.

25. Ibid.

Jackson Pollock deciding to drip paint is not an event. Paint has been dripping since artists have been painting. It is not new, unique, singular, and irreplaceable. It is actually quite ordinary, mundane and boring. The fact that the New York art market choose to see something revolutionary in Pollock's work is a sad testament to a non-creative act posing as revolutionary. Picasso deciding to paint in a Cubist manner is not an event. Children were painting and drawing in this manner long before Picasso claimed it for himself.

Revolutions are not events by their very definition. They revolve around the same old coordinates and demands. The uprisings at Tahir Square in Cairo that toppled the Mubarak regime was not an Event. It was not "shocking, out of joint, appearing to happen all of a sudden."[26] It did not "interrupt the usual flow of things."[27] It was easy to see that the revolution meant business as usual. The same holds for the Occupy Movement.

The American social theorist Cornel West describes the Occupy Movement as a "democratic awakening" yet it is difficult to see any form of democratic awakening coming through the collective tent slumber of its participants. I am sympathetic to certain features of the Occupy Movement namely that Persons should come before profit but I remain perplexed as to how the leaders of this movement plan to change the world by setting up tents in public parks or protesting in front of various City Halls. One should expect more from a group that seeks the total transformation of Western Civilization. Wearing a Che Guevera T-shirt bought at the GAP while using Blackberries and iPhones and then claiming that corporations are the root of all evil is a little more than ironic.

No real coherent message has emerged from this movement, other than we should all wear Guy Fawkes mask to safeguard our anonymity while marching under signs that read, "One Love and "We are the 99%." The Occupy Movement through its very name reveals its inertia. It does not seek the event, it can only "occupy." The movement sets up camp in publicly funded spaces and then is bewildered when the police oust them from their self-declared cities and sites of "participatory democracy." It is clear that the movement thrives when it enacts confrontation with the police. As such, it has no chance of moving past this model.

Some protestors see the movement as a "class war" between the rich and the poor. This idea struck me last week when I was pumping gas. I

26. Ibid., 2.
27. Ibid.

was approached by a youth who said he had just returned from Occupy Toronto and needed money to get back to London. If the young man was an exemplar of the movement then it was clear that the movement was a reactionary circus going nowhere.

The movement rose in popularity only when their encampments were at risk of being taken down by the police. This shows, among other things, that the movement has no real power for positive change. The movement lacks ideological coherence unless chanting, drumming, and playing guitar has become a secret weapon against the forces of capitalism. The concentration of money and power at the top does endanger democracy.

The movement has never openly declared its objectives. Yes, it opposes corporate excess and income inequality but it has not issued a clearly stated manifesto that outlines an alternative model of organizing our social, political and cultural space. This manifesto will never arrive because the movement lacks a foundation. Fighting corporate greed while vandalizing small businesses does not change the mindset of the 1%.

Rather than camp out in tents we could ask and answer the difficult questions such as how do we hold oil companies, big agribusinesses, military contractors, and the pharmaceutical industry who reap billions of dollars of government subsidies and special tax breaks accountable? How do we change our accounting so that poverty and homelessness and other social issues can finally be solved? Can governments begin to cater to the interests of its citizens who are Persons rather than the interests of transnational capital?

Should we believe that those who march the streets to incite global change, have left their jobs and professions, their schools and residences, have risked it all for the greater good? Or does the evidence point to the fact that these protestors are looking for a free ride while not willing or wanting to contribute anything of value to the society that they hold in such contempt?

The Event for Žižek appears mainly in film. Here he gives a number of examples such as the work of Lars Von Trier, David Cronenberg, and Ernst Lubitsch. All we have to do in order to understand the event is to watch *Melancholia, The Tree of Life, M. Butterfly, The Crying Game,* and *Broken Lullaby* while reading Lacan through Hegel.

Žižek holds that for Kierkegaard, "Christianity is the first and only religion of the Event."[28] Apparently, the unique event of the incarnation is

28. Ibid., 38. See http://www.chesterton.org/.

what makes Christianity, well, eventful. However, other religions have the incarnation. Christianity really isn't an event; it is just a footnote to Plato. The Pharaohs of Ancient Egypt were said to be incarnations of the sun gods Horus and Ra. Chinese Emperors, Roman Emperors, even the King of France was thought to be descended from God. Even George Washington is depicted as a god.[29]

Žižek is correct to point out the Patricia Highsmith's short story "Heroine" captures the perversion of Christianity. In the story a mad governess sets fire to the house so she can save the children inside. Malebranche as Žižek points out already had this insight when he showed that God, "wants the others to suffer so that he will be able to help them."[30] God suffers from a kind of Munchausen syndrome by proxy, combined with a Histrionic personality disorder.[31] God the Father watching his Son die on the cross, so he can later be resurrected is the pinnacle of abuse. Žižek quotes the Catholic write G. K. Chesterton who claims, "the glad news brought by the Gospels was the news of original sin."[32] Clearly this is not the good news as Nietzsche already pointed out in his *Anti-Christ*. The good news is that the kingdom of heaven is within you. The good news is the news that we are unique singular and irreducible persons. The notion of original sin is another totalitarian trope that reduces persons to bare life. The narrative is that we should be glad for original sin because now we are in a position to be "saved." In Communist Yugoslavia members of the proletarian brotherhood were allowed to brew alcohol. The regime knew that those who are drunk could not offer much resistance. Those who did not brew their own poison were suspect for their anti-revolutionary activities, because they stood apart from the crowd.

Žižek does say that "the status of subjectivity is eventual"[33] but he cannot think the implications of this Franciscan position further. Instead he claims, "there are three (and only three) key philosophers in the history of western metaphysics: Plato, Descartes and Hegel."[34] The key thinkers

---

29. See https://en.wikipedia.org/wiki/The_Apotheosis_of_Washington and https://en.wikipedia.org/wiki/List_of_people_who_have_been_considered_deities.

30. Žižek, *Event*, 43.

31. See https://www.nlm.nih.gov/medlineplus/ency/article/001555.htm; and https://en.wikipedia.org/wiki/Munchausen_syndrome_by_proxy.

32. Žižek, *Event*, 46.

33. Ibid., 76.

34. Ibid., 77.

of Haecceity that overturn Žižek's triad are Occam, Scotus, and Bonaventure. The thinkers that Žižek sees as key only facilitate a mechanical and mechanistic levelling off of Persons. The Franciscan philosophers, Bonaventure, Scotus, and Ockham became nominalists in order to safeguard each single individual from the power of totalization.

CONCLUSION

Excremental Obfuscation

I sit at the gateway for every rogue, and ask: Who wishes to
deceive me?

—Nietzsche, *Thus Spoke Zarathustra*, "Manly Prudence"

In his article "Psychoanalytic Bullshit," Eugene Brinkema observes,
"As Aristotle implies in his criticism of Heraclitus, the problem is not that
he is lying; but that he is posturing in the guise of philosophizing, with no
regard to the obligations of truth required of that profession. The truth of
bullshit is this affect—utter indifference to the field of truth itself."[1] I take
Brinkema's insight to be an apt summary of Žižek's work.

Harry Frankfurt has shown that there is a phony aspect to bullshit.
Žižek has confessed this phoniness on many occasions. Althusser claimed
that he never read some of the authors he commented on. Did he in fact
actually read Lacan? Do we believe him when he claims that Lacan had provided, "a fantastic philosophy of psychoanalysis that duped everybody."[2] If
Lacan believes he has access to the unconscious then his results should
be clearly stated rather than opaquely played out. If the unconscious dis-
torts our understanding then it will also sabotage our attempt to correct
its distortions, much like drilling a hole for an anchor point in the wall
that has no beams. How have Lacan and Žižek managed to master the

1. Brinkema, "Psychoanalytic Bullshit," 63.
2. Kirschner, "The Man Who Didn't Exist," 228.

unconscious other than with prose that makes little sense and solutions that are monstrous.

What can be concluded from Žižek's authorship? What we have in Žižek's work is the imaginings of Hegel filtered through the obfuscations of Lacan in order to read culture. Rather than turn to Lacanian psychoanalysis to solve our problems, the obvious answer is eHarmony.com. This site uses algorithm's to match couples on the basis of "deep compatibility." This site coupled with fashion guru Gok Wan's advice should be enough to escape from the primordial horror which is the source of our jouissance. Then we can be free to really watch *The Simpsons* and conclude that Maggie Simpson's soother is the Real that really should be in Homer's mouth. And then? What do I do with such earth shattering revelations whose shockwaves reverberate through the corridors of cultural studies departments in California—the state of theory as Derrida liked to point out?

In his interview with Rasmussen, Žižek reveals the punch line to his work. The passage is worth quoting in full. Žižek says, "If you were to ask me at gunpoint . . . what are you really trying to do? I would say, Screw ideology, screw movie analysis . . . Let me give you a metaphoric formula. You know the term Deleuze uses for reading philosophers—anal interpretation, buggering them. Deleuze says that in contrast to other interpreters, he anally penetrates the philosopher because its immaculate conception. You produce a monster. I'm trying to do what Deleuze forgot to do—to bugger Hegel with Lacan so that you get a monstrous Hegel which is for me precisely the underlying radical dimension of subjectivity. It's a very technical, modest project but I believe in it."[3] Here we finally learn what Žižek wants. We learn his truth. He is "buggering" Hegel with Lacan.[4] What the students at Vincennes said to Lacan applies equally to Žižek: "Up there to the right of God, that's Lacan. What is a master? It's Lacan . . . It's true that you are a fine and famous clown."[5]

While Žižek wants to resurrect the legacy of German Idealism, we should guard against it. We must fight against the Hegelianism that kills the individual while glorifying death. Recall Hegel's words from the *Phenomenology of Spirit*: "The sole work and dead of universal freedom is death . . . .it is the coldest and meanest of deaths with no more significance than

3. Rasmussen, "Liberation Hurts: An Interview with Slavoj Žižek."
4. This phrase comes from Johnston, *Žižek's Ontology*, 126.
5. Lacan, "Impromtu at Vincennes," 127.

cutting off the head of a cabbage or swallowing a mouthful of water."[6] When Žižek wants to reactivate his technically modest project we must put such idealism to sleep. Hegel writes,

"The life of Spirit is not the life that shrinks from death and keeps itself untouched by devastation, but rather the life that endures it and maintains itself in it . . . it runs its truth only when, in utter dismemberment it finds itself."[7] What is left after "utter dismemberment"? Does one become like the Knight in the Monty Python film who declares that his lost limbs are only little flesh wounds?

Paul Hollander's insights are clear. He writes, "Žižek personifies the confused longing for meaning, social solidarity and utopian fulfillment to be achieved by bold, cleansing violence that permeated totalitarian movements and systems of the past century. Intellectual historians of the future will not find it easy to explain why these longings and their incoherent expression made him a celebrity but they will probably recognize that he embodied and expressed many dubious cultural and political currents of our times."[8]

Let us take Žižek's understanding of the refugee crisis in Europe as an example of his politics in practice. Žižek begins with the Hegelian insights that the refugees from Africa and the Middle East into Western Europe constitute a "flow." He claims that the reactions this "flow" have produced in Europe are "strikingly similar to those we display on learning we have a terminal illness, according to the schema described by Elisabeth Kubler-Ross in her classic study *On Death*."[9] Here Žižek is reaching for analogies that make no sense but in a deep way reveal his position toward the Other. The refuges who "flow" into Europe are like cancer. Refugees are de-humanized when they are described as a flow, an influx, a flood, a wave, and a stream that threatens Europe's "legitimate" body with danger. The language used by Žižek is as de-humanizing as Kubler-Ross's easy schema that maintains all I have to do to come to terms with death is go through a Hegelian dialectic that leads from denial, anger, bargaining, depression, and finally acceptance of my situation.

In his analysis of the refugee crisis, Žižek fails to see what is at stake, namely, the irreducibility of persons. The individual bodies that washed up on the Greek beaches show us that we have not acted on time. What

6. Hegel, *Phenomenology of Spirit*, S 20.

7. Ibid., S 32.

8. Hollander, "Slavoj Žižek and the Rise of the Celebrity Intellectual," 360.

9. Žižek, "The Non-Existence of Norway."

Žižek fails to mention is that a vast majority of the Syrian refugees reaching Europe are middle class and secular. That is to say, their values and way of life are not that different from middle-class Europeans. What is Žižek's conclusion? "Refuges are the price we pay for a globalised economy in which commodities—but not people—are permitted to circulate freely."[10] Notice how Žižek the master Lacanian-Hegelian-Stalinist theoretician of *Kung-Fu Panda*, Soviet jokes, and Hitchcock, embraces the very Capitalism he seeks to overturn.

Human life is calculated in terms of cost, benefit and price rather than personal value. The claim is, that refugees are, a drain on the already withering capitalist system that sees bankers, and industrialists fatten up like the hoarding farmers in Roald Dahl's *Fantastic Mr. Fox,* while the unfortunate masses get herded into refugee camps and wash up dead on Europe's pristine beaches. But hey, life is not fair. Žižek's article in the *London Review of Books*, speaks to the ruling class, to European bureaucrats in Brussels. He tells them what they already know. They are masters at imposing rules and regulations; for legalizing repressive measures. Žižek says that, "Europe must reassert its commitment to provide for the dignified treatment of refugees."[11] The obvious question is when did Europe ever assert its commitment for the dignified treatment of refugees? Žižek says that European rules "should be clearly stated and enforced by repressive measures."[12] This stance is what Derrida would call a crime of hospitality. Instead of seeing the ethical implications in Derrida's thought, Žižek concludes by stating that communism needs to be reinvented. "Maybe this is, in the long term, the only solution."[13] To this I say, "No Thanks!"

Žižek's fall back answer is to turn to Hegel. In his inaugural address delivered at the University of Berlin on October 22, 1818, Hegel defends the interest of the State. He writes, "And it is this state in particular, the state which has taken me into its midst, which, by virtue of its spiritual supremacy, has raised itself to its present importance in actuality and in the political realm, and has made itself the equal in power and independence, of those states which may surpass it in external resources . . . What is true, great and divine in life is so by virtue of the Idea; the goal of

10. Ibid.
11. Ibid.
12. Ibid.
13. Ibid.

philosophy is to grasp the Idea in its true shape and universality."[14] Here we clearly see the line that Žižek follows in reducing the singular person to a universal abstraction.

Hegel is correct when he writes, "To do nothing when the ground shakes beneath our feet but wait blindly and cheerfully for the collapse of the old building which is full of cracks and rotten to its foundations, and to let oneself be crushed by the falling timbers, is as contrary to prudence as it is to honour."[15] But Hegel does not valorize the person. He wants to set up a better Institution so that the Spirit can return to dwell there. He is not interested in the sanctity of persons. His speeches to use his own words, "conceal the gravediggers behind a screen of fine words."[16]

To use Derrida's words, we have faith in the "singularity which displaces, undoes the social bond, and replays it otherwise."[17] It is not the case that the universal must always be attained through the particular. Rather, it is the particular that must attain its haecceity. When Amy Hollywood asks, "What is the new Event in the face of which we are called to act?"[18] the answer is clear. We do not turn to the potency of Christ's resurrection, but to the potency of our own haecceity that is incarnated within each of us.

In his article for *Newsweek* explaining the impact of the recently released *Panama Papers*, Žižek writes, "the only truly surprising thing about the *Panama Papers* leak is that there is no surprise in them."[19] We have always known that the ultra-rich hide their money. The fact that we still allow it to happen after 10,000 years of culture is more than a little surprising. The "existing global order" has not changed. We tolerate the power of others over us. We prefer to kneel down rather than to make a stand.

Žižek asks, "But what we should do is change the topic immediately from morality to our economic system: politicians, bankers and managers

14. Hegel, "Inaugural Address, Delivered at the University of Berlin." Hegel's address needs to be compared with Heidegger's inaugural address at the University of Freiburg when he became Rektor. Heidegger echoes Hegel's claims when he writes, "The will to the essence of the German university is the will to science as will to the historical mission of the German people as a people that knows itself in its state. Together, science and German fate must come to power in this will to essence." Heidegger's thought cannot think the Person. Dasein is not a singular Person.

15. Hegel, "The Magistrates Should Be Elected by the People," 2.

16. Ibid.

17. Derrida, "Cinema and its Ghosts: An Interview with Jacques Derrida," 29.

18. Hollywood, "Saint Paul and the New Man," 8761.

19. Zizek, "Explaining the Panama Papers or Why Does a Dog Lick Himself."

were always greedy, so what is it in our legal and economic system that enable them to realize their greed in such a big way?"[20]

It is clear that high level politicians, bankers, accountants, lawyers, managers, in short all the Pharaoh's administrators set up a game in which they win at every turn. Even when they lose they never have to pay. As the 2008 financial meltdown showed, they all play with loaded dice. Yes, Žižek is correct. "Corruption is not a contingent deviation of the global capitalist system, it is part of its basic functioning."[21] The question he does not answer is why do we allow the game to continue?

Žižek sees the Papers as evidence of a class division. He writes, "the papers demonstrate how wealthy people live in a separate world in which different rules apply, in which legal systems and police authority are heavily trusted and not only protect the rich, but are even ready to systematically bend the rules of law to accommodate them."[22] Our global system is "corruption legalized."

But Žižek's conclusion in the form of "the old vulgar riddle-joke," Why do dogs lick themselves? "Because they can" is wrong. Dogs lick themselves because they are dogs. The question, "Why do humans choose to be sheep?" requires an answer that communism and capitalism cannot provide.

Present talk about equality and democracy remain for Derrida, "little more than an obscene alibi so long as it tolerates the terrible plight of so many millions of human beings suffering from malnutrition, disease, humiliation grossly deprived of not only bread and water, but of equality and freedom, dispossesses of the rights of all, of everyone, of anyone."[23]

Following the Franciscans, Derrida speaks of that "incalculable element that must be left to birth, to the coming to light, into the word of a unique, irreplaceable, free and thus non-programmable living being."[24]

I am reminded here of a painting by Goya entitled, "The Half-Sunken Dog" (El Perro Semihundido). The painting portrays a dog half buried in yellow sand. Instead of seeing the animal as sinking in the quick sand and the holy promises of globalization, I can overcome my pessimism and view the painting as a scene of transformation—the wolf emerges from its domestication to become what it is. It emerges to resist classification.

20. Ibid.
21. Ibid.
22. Ibid.
23. Derrida, *Rogues*, 86.
24. Ibid.

This Eucharistic wolf is hostis: stranger, enemy, and victim unable to be received by the dogs of civilization who hound it with identity tags.

Derrida calls us to think from a larger perspective, past human parameters with a giving that gives without submission.

Are we asking too much of philosophy when we expect it to finally give birth to an event that would transform the coordinates of our entrenched positions?

Can there be a step outside of the legacy we have inherited that would not only radically transform the state of things, but also more importantly allow justice to happen?

I fear the opposite will happen; little dictators riding horses or Lear jets, will always seduce Nietzsche's little man. Rather than justice, CEOs who ride on the backs and minds of the masses into entrepreneurial bliss will be praised for their blackberry wisdom, packaged ready-made like six ply toilet paper that never suffers from a recession or a downturn in consumer confidence because the space of its utilization never changes.

The wolf is brought into the city and made a member of the household. Heimlich means home but it can also mean, hidden, secret, and dangerous. Is this the reason the wolf is punished for being a rogue? It is too intimate, it knows our weakness.

It knows that the fat we hide behind in such excessive amounts was accumulated through murder and crimes of hospitality.

It knows the shame we carry as humans, as the animals that we are, namely that we are a species that loves to eat its own in so many different ways.

Are we not this thing that devours the irreducible so that no trace of our transgressions remain?

According to legend, from the cross at San Damiano, Jesus said to Francis, "Repair my house, which is falling into ruin." Jesus told Francis to repair the *nosmos* of haecceity, not the *nosmos* of economy.

Žižek declares that his monstrous Hegel "buggered" by Lacan, (posing as Žižek of course), brings us to "the underlying radical dimension of subjectivity." It does not. Žižek like Hegel can lead us only to the gulag. Žižek's excremental member leads only to the death drive. A Hegel who saw little Napoleon on his horse as the embodiment of the Absolute Geist can offer us nothing today. Neither can Žižek.[25]

---

25. This insight does not stop the Žižek machine from putting out more congratulatory texts. See for example, Hamza, *Repeating Žižek*. This text of collected essays appears in a series edited by Slavoj Žižek.

Bibliography

Adorno, Theodor W. *An Introduction to Dialectics*. Translated by Nicholas Walker. Edited by Christoph Ziermann. Malden, MA: Polity, 2017.

Althusser, Louis. *On Ideology*. London: Verso, 2008.

Baumann, Zygmunt. "On Consumers Coming Home to Roost." *Social Europe* 9, August 9, 2011.

Berger, Claudia. "The Leader's Two Bodies." *Diacritics* 31, no. 1 (2001) 73–90

Bielik-Robson, Agata. "The Promise of the Name: 'Jewish Nominalism' as the Critique of Idealist Tradition." *Bamidbar* 1.3 (2012) 11–35.

Bijelić, Dušan. "'Immigrants as the Enemy: Psychoanalysis and the Balkans' Self-Orientalization." *Slavonic and East European Review* 87, no. 3 (2009) 488–517.

Bordwell, David. "Slavoj Žižek: Say Anything." Online at http://www.davidbordwell.net/essays/zizek.php.

Brinkema, Eugene. "Psychoanalytic Bullshit." *Journal of Speculative Philosophy*. N.S., 21, no. 1 (2007) 61–79.

Butler, Rex, ed. *The Žižek Dictionary*. New York: Routledge, 2014.

Cohen, Nick. Review of *Revolution* by Russell Brand: The Barmy Credo of a Beverly Hills Buddhist. *Observer*, October 26, 2014.

Castoriadis, Corneliuis. *Crossroads in the Labyrinth*. Translated by Kate Soper and Martin H. Ryle. Sussex: Harvester, 1984.

Chesterton, G. K. *The Collected Works of G. K. Chesterton*. Vol. 4. San Francisco: Ignatius, 1987.

———. *What's Wrong with the World*. New York: Dodd, Mead, 1910.

Chiesa, Lorenzo. *Subjectivity and Otherness: A Philosophical Reading of Lacan*. Cambridge, MA: MIT Press, 2007.

Cohen, Nick. "Revolution by Russell Brand review—The Barmy Credo of a Beverly Hills Buddhist." The Guardian (October 26, 2014). Online at http://www.theguardian.com/books/2014/oct/27/revolution-review-russell-brand-beverly-hills-buddhist.

Dean, Jodi. "Re-Politicizing the Left." *Minnesota Review* 81 (2013) 79–101.

Derrida, Jacques. "Cinema and Its Ghosts: An Interview with Jacques Derrida." *Discourse* 37, nos. 1–2 (2015) 29.

———. *Politics of Friendship*. Translated by George Collins. Phronesis. London: Verso, 1997.

———. *Rogues: Two Essays on Reason*. Translated by Pascale-Anne Brault and Michael Naas. Stanford, CA: Stanford University Press, 2005.

de Sutter, Laurent, ed. *Žižek and the Law*. New York: Routledge, 2015.

Eagleton, Terry. "Method in the madness: The Ticklish Subject." *Times Higher Education* (November 19, 1999). Online at https://www.timeshighereducation.com/books/method-in-the-madness/157391.article.

Edwards, Lee. "The Legacy of Mao Zedong is Mass Murder." The Heritage Foundation. Online at https://www.heritage.org/asia/commentary/the-legacy-mao-zedong-mass-murder.

Esposito, Roberto. "The Metapolitical Structure of the West." Translated by Matt Langione. *Qui Parle* 22, no.2 (2014) 147–61.

Fackenheim, Emil. "On the Actuality of the Rational and the Rationality of the Actual." *Review of Metaphysics* 23, no. 4 (1970) 690–98.

Fanon, Frantz. *Black Skin, White Mask*. New York: Grove, 2008.

Fichte, Johann Gottlieb. *The Science of Knowledge (Wissenschaftslehre)*. Translated by Peter Lauchlan Heath and John Lachs. New York: Appleton-Century-Crofts, 1970.

Hart, William David. "Can a Judgment Be Read? A Response to Slavoj Žižek." *Nepantla* 4, no. 1 (2003) 191–94.

Hegel, G. W. F. "Jenaer Realphilosophie." In *Frühe politische Systeme*. Frankfurt: Ullstein, 1974.

———. *Lectures on Logic: Berlin, 1831*. Translated by Clark Butler. Bloomington: Indiana University Press, 2008.

———. *Phenomenology of Mind*. 2 vols. Translated by J. B. Baillie. New York: Cosimo Classics, 2005.

———. *Philosophy of Right*. Translated by T. M. Knox. Oxford: Oxford University Press, 1955.

———. *Science of Logic*. Translated by A. V. Miller. London: Allen & Unwin, 1969.

Hollander, Paul. "Slavoj Žižek and the Rise of the Celebrity Intellectual." *SOC* 47, no. 4 (2010) 47.

Hollywood, Amy. "Saint Paul and the New Man." *Critical Inquiry* 35, no. 4 (2009) 865–76.

Jagodzinski, Jan. "Struggling with Žižek's Ideology: The Deleuzian Complaint, Or, Why Is Žižek a Disguised Deleuzian in Denial?" *International Journal of Žižek Studies* 4, no. 1 (2010) 1–24.

Johnson, Alan. "The Ruthless Mind of Slavoj Žižek." *Dissent* (2009) 122–27.

Johnston, Adrian. *Žižek's Ontology: A Transcendental Materialist Theory of Subjectivity*. Northwestern University Studies in Phenomenology and Existential Philosophy. Evanston, IL: Northwestern University Press, 2008.

Kant, Immanuel. *The Critique of Pure Reason*. Translated by Paul Guyer. Cambridge: Cambridge University Press, 1997.

Kierkegaard, Søren. *The Concept of Anxiety*. Translated by Reidar Thomte. Kierkegaard's Writings 8. Princeton: Princeton University Press, 1980.

———. *Concluding Unscientific PostScript to Philosophical Fragments*. Vol. 1. Edited and translated by Howard V. Hong and Edna H. Hong. Kierkegaard's Writings 12. Princeton: Princeton University Press, 1992.

———. *Fear and Trembling/Repetition*. Edited and translated by Howard V. Hong and Edna H. Hong. Kierkegaard's Writings 6. Princeton: Princeton University Press, 1983.

———. *The Point of View for My Work as an Author: A Report to History*. Translated by Walter Lowrie. New York: Harper, 1962.

———. *Sickness unto Death*. Edited and translated by Howard V. Hong and Edna H. Hong. Kierkegaard's Writings 19. Princeton: Princeton University Press, 1983.

———. *The Soul of Kierkegaard: Selections from His Journal*. Edited with an introduction by Alexander Dru. Mineola, NY: Dover, 2003.

———. *Two Ages*. Translated by Howard V. Hong and Edna H. Hong, Kierkegaard's Writings 14. Princeton: Princeton University Press, 1978.

———. *Works of Love*. Edited and translated by Howard V. Hong and Edna H. Hong. Kierkegaard's Writings 16. Princeton: Princeton University Press, 1995.

Kirsch, Adam. "The Deadly Jester." *New Republic*, November 25, 2008.

Kirshner, Lewis A. "The Man Who Didn't Exist: The Case of Louis Althusser." *American Imago* 60:2 (Summer 2003) 211–39.

Lacan Jacques. *Seminar XI: The Four Fundamental Concepts of Psychoanalysis*. Edited by Jacques-Alain Miller. Translated by Alan Sheridan. London: Hogarth, 1977.

Laclau, Ernesto. *Contingency, Hegemony, Universality: Contemporary Dialogues on the Left*. London: Verso, 2000.

———. "Why Constructing a People is the Main Task of Politics." *Critical Inquiry* 32.4 (Summer 2006) 646–80.

Laing, R. D. *The Politics of Experience and The Bird of Paradise*. London: Penguin, 1967.

Lenin, V. I. "Lessons of the Moscow Uprising." Proletary 2 (August 29, 1906). Online at https://www.marxists.org/archive/lenin/works/1906/aug/29.htm.

Linton, Marisa. "Robespierre and the Terror." *History Today* 56, no. 8 (2006) 23–29.

Marx, Karl. "Kritische Randglossen zu dem Artikel 'Der König von Preussen und die Sozialreform. Von einem Preussen." In vol. 1 of *Werke* by Karl Marx and Friedrich Engels, 392–409. Berlin: Dietz Verlag, 1958.

Mbembe, Achille. "Necropolitics." *Public Culture* 15, no. 1 (2003) 11–40.

Mueller, John P., and William J. Richardson. *A Reader's Guide to "Ecrits."* New York: International Universities Press, 1994.

Nietzsche, Friedrich. *Basic Writings of Nietzsche*. Translated and edited by Walter Kaufmann. Introduction by Peter Gay. The Modern Library Classics. New York: The Modern Library, 2000.

———. *Thus Spoke Zarathustra*. Translated by R. J. Hollingdale. New York: Penguin Books, 1999.

Olson, Gary, and Lynn Worsham. "Slavoj Žižek: Philosopher, Cultural Critic and Cyber-Communist." *JAC* 21, no. 2 (2001) 251–86.

Parker, Ian. Review of *Žižek's Politics*, by Jodi Dean. *Ephemera* 7, no. 3 (2007) 481–84.

Pickus, David. "Did Somebody Evade Totalitarianism? On the Intellectual Escapism of Slavoj Žižek." *Humanitas* 21, nos. 1–2 (2008) 146–67.

Punj, Balbir K. "The Time Has Come to Bury Lenin." *The Pioneer* (October 21, 2005). Online at http://www.hvk.org/2005/1105/64.html.

Rancière, Jacques. *Disagreement, Politics and Philosophy*. University of Minnesota Press, 1999.

———. *On the Shores of Politics*. New York: Verso, 1995.

———. *The Philosopher and His Poor*. Durham, NC: Duke University Press, 2003.

Bibliography

————. "Ten Theses on Politics." Translated by Rachael Bowlby and Davide Panagia. *Theory and Event* 5, no. 3 (2001). DOI: 10.1353/tae.2001.0028.

Russell, Bertrand. *Unpopular Essays*. New York: Schuster, 1964.

Schmidt, Carl. *Political Theology: Four Chapters on the Concept of Sovereignty*. Cambridge: MIT Press, 1985.

Sharpe, Matthew. *Žižek and Politics: A Critical Introduction*. Edinburgh: University of Edinburgh Press, 2010.

Taylor, Paul. "Žižek's Brand of Philosophical Excess and the Treason of Intellectuals." *Comparatist* 38 (2014) 128–47.

Tebbutt, Suzanne. *An Examination of Kierkegaard's Existential Faith*. Cologne: LAP, 2011.

Temple, Emily. "'The Literary Equivalent of a Big Mac': Self-Deprecating Quips from Authors." The Atlantic (December 26, 2012). Online at https://www.theatlantic.com/entertainment/archive/2012/12/the-literary-equivalent-of-a-big-mac-self-deprecating-quips-from-authors/266476/.

Unamuno, Miguel de. *Abel Sanchez and Other Stories*. New York: Regnery, 1956.

West, Cornel, *Democracy Matters*. New York: Penguin, 2004.

Žižek, Slavoj. *Absolute Recoil: Towards a New Foundation of Dialectical Materialism*. London: Verso, 2014.

————. "The Big Other Doesn't Exist." *Journal of European Psychoanlysis* (Spring-Fall 1997). Online at http://www.lacan.com/zizekother.htm.

————. "Critical Response I: A Symptom—of What?" Critical Inquiry 29:3 (Spring 2003) 486–503.

————. *Demanding the Impossible*. Malden, MA: Polity, 2013.

————. *Did Somebody Say Totalitarianism?* London: Verso, 2001.

————. *Enjoy Your Symptom!* London: Routledge, 1992.

————. *Event: A Philosophical Journey Through a Concept*. New York: Penguin, 2014.

————. "Explaining the Panama Papers or Why Does a Dog Lick Himself." *Newseek*, March 7, 2016.

————. *First As Tragedy, Then As Farce*. London: Verso, 2009.

————. *For They Know Not What They Do*. London: Verso, 1991.

————. *The Fragile Absolute: Or, Why is the Christian Legacy Worth Fighting For?* London: Verso, 2000.

————. *The Fright of Real Tears*. London: British Film Institute (BFI), 2001.

————. *How to Read Lacan*. London: Granta, 2006.

————. "Human Rights and Its Discontents." November 15, 1999. Bard College. http://www.lacan.com/zizek-human.htm.

————. *In Defense of Lost Causes*. London: Verso, 2008.

————. *Interrogating the Real*. Edited by Rex Butler and Scott Stephens. New York: Continuum, 2006.

————. *Iraq: The Borrowed Kettle*. London: Verso, 2004.

————, ed. *Lacan: The Silent Partners*. London: Verso, 2006.

————. *Less Than Nothing: Hegel and the Shadow of Dialectical Materialism*. London: Verso, 2013.

————. *Living in the End Times*. London: Verso, 2010.

————. *Looking Awry*. Cambridge, MA: MIT Press, 1991.

————. *The Metastases of Enjoyment*. London: Verso, 1994.

————. *On Belief*. London: Routledge, 2001.

———. "Only a Suffering God Can Save Us: Section 2: Kierkegaard." Online at http://www.lacan.com/zizmarqueemoon.html.

———. *Organs without Bodies*. London: Routledge, 2003.

———. *The Parallax View*. Cambridge, MA: MIT Press, 2006.

———. *The Plague of Fantasies*. London: Verso. 1997.

———. *The Puppet and the Dwarf: The Perverse Core of Christianity*. Cambridge, MA: MIT Press, 2003.

———. *Repeating Lenin*. Zagreb: Arkzin D.O.O., 2001.

———. "Repeating Lenin—Lenin's Choice." Online at https://www.marxists.org/reference/subject/philosophy/works/ot/zizek1.htm.

———. *Revolution at the Gates: Žižek on Lenin, the 1917 Writings*. London: Verso, 2002.

———. *The Sublime Object of Ideology*. London: Verso, 1989.

———. *Tarrying With the Negative*. Durham, NC: Duke University Press, 1993.

———. "Tibet: Dream and Reality." *Le Monde diplomatique* (May 2008). Online at https://mondediplo.com/2008/05/09tibet.

———. *The Ticklish Subject*. London: Verso, 1999.

———. *Trouble in Paradise: From the End of History to the End of Capitalism*. London: Allen Lane, 2014.

———. "20 Years of Collapse." *The New York Times* (November 9, 2009) A23. Online at https://www.nytimes.com/2009/11/09/opinion/09zizek.html.

———. *The Universal Exception*. Edited by Rex Butler and Scott Stephens. London: Bloomsbury, 2006.

———. *Violence: Six Sideways Reflections*. Big Ideas/Small Books. New York: Picador, 2008.

———. *Welcome to the Desert of the Real*. London: Verso, 2002.

———. "What Is to be Done (with Lenin)?" In These Time (January 21, 2004). Online at http://www.lacan.com/zizeklenin34.htm.

———. "What to Do When Evil Is Dancing on the Ruins of Evil." *Positions: East Asia Cultures Critique* 19, no. 3 (2011) 653–69.

Žižek, Slavoj, and John Milbank. *The Monstrosity of Christ: Paradox or Dialectic?* Edited by Creston Davis. Cambridge, MA: The MIT Press, 2009.

Žižek, Slavoj, Eric L. Santner, and Kenneth Reinhard. *The Neighbor: Three Inquiries in Political Theology*. 2nd ed. Chicago: University of Chicago Press, 2013.

www.ingramcontent.com/pod-product-compliance
Lightning Source LLC
Chambersburg PA
CBHW070924270326
41927CB00011B/2710